Reading Link

Robert Hickling

Misato Usukura

KINSEIDO

Kinseido Publishing Co., Ltd.

3-21 Kanda Jimbo-cho, Chiyoda-ku,
Tokyo 101-0051, Japan

First published 2020 by Kinseido Publishing Co., Ltd.

Design   Nampoosha Co., Ltd.
Illustrations   Miyuki Suzuki

Acknowledgment
Robert Hickling would like to express his special thanks to his wife for all of her support.

 音声ファイル無料ダウンロード

https://www.kinsei-do.co.jp/download/4100

この教科書で DL 00 の表示がある箇所の音声は、上記 URL または QR コードにて
無料でダウンロードできます。自習用音声としてご活用ください。

- ▶ PC からのダウンロードをお勧めします。スマートフォンなどでダウンロードされる場合は、
  ダウンロード前に「解凍アプリ」をインストールしてください。
- ▶ URL は、**検索ボックスではなくアドレスバー (URL 表示欄)** に入力してください。
- ▶ お使いのネットワーク環境によっては、ダウンロードできない場合があります。

◎ CD 00　左記の表示がある箇所の音声は、教室用 CD (Class Audio CD) に収録されています。

はしがき

*Reading Link*は段階的に学習できるように構成されたリーディング中心の教科書です。語彙の確認から始まり、短めの文章を読んでざっくりと内容理解をした後、同じトピックについて書かれた長めの文章を、質問に答えたりサマリーチャートを完成させたりしながら読み進めます。大学生の知的好奇心を刺激する題材と、内容理解を促す付属タスクにより、英語が苦手な学生であっても、あきらめずに学習を続けることができます。各ユニットは6ページで構成されています。各ユニットの構成は次のようになっています。

Words to Pictures

Tune-Up Readingに登場する重要な語彙の意味を確認します。（2〜3分）

Tune-Up Reading

短めの英文（60〜70語程度）を読み、Ｔ／Ｆ問題に答えます。（5分）

Grammar Basics

ターゲットとなる文法項目を、豊富な例文と簡潔な日本語の説明で学びます。（10分）

 Tune-Up Readingの英文の中から、Grammar Basicsで取り上げた文法項目を探して下線を引く活動です。文脈の中で文法を学ぶことを目指しています。（5分）

Grammar Practice

Ａ 選択肢式の文法練習問題（8問）です。（10分）

Ｂ 文法項目への理解を確かにするための練習問題です。ここでは、主に和文英訳問題（2問）に取り組みます。（10分）

Prepare to Read

Enjoy Readingに登場する重要な語彙の意味を確認します。（5分）

Enjoy Reading

A 長めの英文（180語程度）を読んで、大まかな内容理解を問う質問（3問）に答えます。答えに当たる箇所を本文中から探して下線を引く形式で答えます。（5分）

B 英文をもう一度読んで、サマリーチャートを完成させます。英語のサマリーチャート内の空所に入る語句を、選択肢の中から選んで答えます。（10分）

C 英文の内容に関して書かれた3つの記述について、記述文の空所に入る語句を選択肢の中から選んで答えます。**A** **B** のタスクで取り上げられた箇所とはできるだけ重複しないようになっています。（5分）

Word Collector

A イラストと単語を結び付けながら、ユニットのトピックに関連する語彙をさらに学びます。（5分）

B **A** で学んだ語彙とユニットで学んだ文法項目を使って、文脈の中で語彙を使う練習をします。文中に適切な単語を入れる穴埋め形式のタスクや、語句の並べ替え英作文、間違い探しなど、ユニットによって形式はさまざまです。（5分）

最後に、本書の作成にあたり、金星堂の皆様から多くのご助言、ご支援をいただいただけでなく、多大なご尽力を賜りました。この場をお借りして御礼申し上げます。

著者一同

本書は CheckLink（チェックリンク）対応テキストです。

CheckLinkのアイコンが表示されている設問は、CheckLinkに対応しています。

CheckLinkを使用しなくても従来通りの授業ができますが、特色をご理解いただき、授業活性化のためにぜひご活用ください。

CheckLinkの特色について

大掛かりで複雑な従来のe-learningシステムとは異なり、CheckLinkのシステムは大きな特色として次の3点が挙げられます。

1. これまで行われてきた教科書を使った授業展開に大幅な変化を加えることなく、専門的な知識なしにデジタル学習環境を導入することができる。
2. PC教室やCALL教室といった最新の機器が導入された教室に限定されることなく、普通教室を使用した授業でもデジタル学習環境を導入することができる。
3. 授業中での使用に特化し、教師・学習者双方のモチベーション・集中力をアップさせ、授業自体を活性化することができる。

▶教科書を使用した授業に「デジタル学習環境」を導入できる

本システムでは、学習者は教科書のCheckLinkのアイコンが表示されている設問にPCやスマートフォン、携帯電話端末からインターネットを通して解答します。そして教師は、授業中にリアルタイムで解答結果を把握し、正解率などに応じて有効な解説を行うことができるようになっています。教科書自体は従来と何ら変わりはありません。解答の手段としてCheckLinkを使用しない場合でも、従来通りの教科書として使用して授業を行うことも、もちろん可能です。

▶教室環境を選ばない

従来の多機能なe-learning教材のように学習者側の画面に多くの機能を持たせることはせず、「解答する」ことに機能を特化しました。PCだけでなく、一部タブレット端末やスマートフォン、携帯電話端末からの解答も可能です。したがって、PC教室やCALL教室といった大掛かりな教室は必要としません。普通教室でもCheckLinkを用いた授業が可能です。教師はPCだけでなく、一部タブレット端末やスマートフォンからも解答結果の確認をすることができます。

▶授業を活性化するための支援システム

本システムは予習や復習のツールとしてではなく、授業中に活用されることで真価を発揮する仕組みになっています。CheckLinkというデジタル学習環境を通じ、教師と学習者双方が授業中に解答状況などの様々な情報を共有することで、学習者はやる気を持って解答、教師は解答状況に応じて効果的な解説を行う、という好循環を生み出します。CheckLinkは、普段の授業をより活力のあるものへと変えていきます。

上記3つの大きな特色以外にも、掲示板などの授業中に活用できる機能を用意しています。従来通りの教科書としても使用はできますが、ぜひCheckLinkの機能をご理解いただき、普段の授業をより活性化されたものにしていくためにご活用ください。

CheckLink の使い方

CheckLinkは、PCや一部タブレット端末、スマートフォン、携帯電話端末を用いて、この教科書の
↻CheckLink のアイコン表示のある設問に解答するシステムです。
・初めてCheckLinkを使う場合、以下の要領で**「学習者登録」**と**「教科書登録」**を行います。
・一度登録を済ませれば、あとは毎回**「ログイン画面」**から入るだけです。CheckLinkを使う
　教科書が増えたときだけ、改めて**「教科書登録」**を行ってください。

CheckLink URL

https://checklink.kinsei-do.co.jp/student/

QRコードの読み取り
ができる端末の場合は
こちらから ▶▶▶

ご注意ください！ 上記URLは**「検索ボックス」**でなく**「アドレスバー(URL表示欄)」**に入力してください。

▶学習者登録

①上記URLにアクセスすると、右のページが表示されます。学校名を入力
　し「ログイン画面へ」をクリックしてください。
　PCの場合は「PC用はこちら」をクリックしてPC用ページを表示します。
　同様に学校名を入力し「ログイン画面へ」をクリックしてください。
②ログイン画面が表示されたら**「初めての方はこちら」**をクリックし
　「学習者登録画面」に入ります。

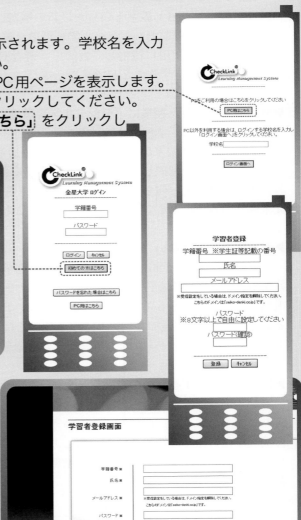

③自分の学籍番号、氏名、メールアドレス(学校
　のメールなど**PCメールを推奨**)を入力し、次
　に**任意のパスワード**を8桁以上20桁未満(半
　角英数字)で入力します。なお、学籍番号は
　パスワードとして使用することはできません。
④「パスワード確認」は、❸で入力したパスワー
　ドと同じものを入力します。
⑤最後に「登録」ボタンをクリックして登録は
　完了です。次回からは、「ログイン画面」から
　学籍番号とパスワードを入力してログインし
　てください。

▶教科書登録

①ログイン後、メニュー画面から「教科書登録」を選び（PCの場合はその後「新規登録」ボタンをクリック）、「教科書登録」画面を開きます。

②教科書と受講する授業を登録します。
教科書の最終ページにある、**教科書固有番号**のシールをはがし、印字された**16桁の数字とアルファベット**を入力します。

③授業を担当される先生から連絡された**11桁の授業ID**を入力します。

④最後に「登録」ボタンをクリックして登録は完了です。

⑤実際に使用する際は「教科書一覧」（PCの場合は「教科書選択画面」）の該当する教科書名をクリックすると、「問題解答」の画面が表示されます。

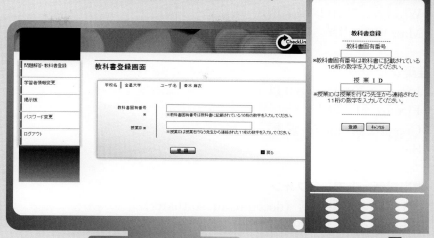

▶問題解答

①問題は教科書を見ながら解答します。この教科書の ⟳CheckLink のアイコン表示のある設問に解答できます。

②問題が表示されたら選択肢を選びます。

③表示されている問題に解答した後、「解答」ボタンをクリックすると解答が登録されます。

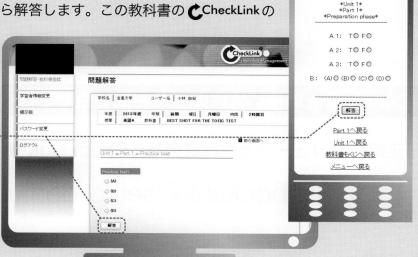

▶CheckLink 推奨環境

PC

推奨 OS
  Windows 7, 10 以降
  MacOS X 以降

推奨ブラウザ
  Internet Explorer 8.0 以上
  Firefox 40.0 以上
  Google Chrome 50 以上
  Safari

携帯電話・スマートフォン
  3G 以降の携帯電話（docomo, au, softbank）
  iPhone, iPad（iOS9 〜）
  Android OS スマートフォン、タブレット

・最新の推奨環境についてはウェブサイトをご確認ください。
・上記の推奨環境を満たしている場合でも、機種によってはご利用いただけない場合もあります。また、推奨環境は技術動向等により変更される場合があります。

▶CheckLink 開発

CheckLink は奥田裕司 福岡大学教授、正興 IT ソリューション株式会社、株式会社金星堂によって共同開発されました。

CheckLink は株式会社金星堂の登録商標です。

CheckLink の使い方に関するお問い合わせは…

正興ITソリューション株式会社　CheckLink 係

e-mail checklink@seiko-denki.co.jp

Reading Link

Who Is Pepper?

現在形

次のイラストに合う語句をa〜dから選びましょう。　CheckLink　DL 02　CD 02

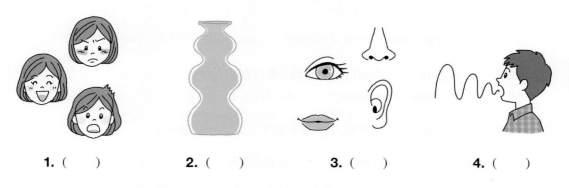

1. (　　)　　　**2.** (　　)　　　**3.** (　　)　　　**4.** (　　)

a. curvy design　　**b.** expressions　　**c.** voice tone　　**d.** facial features

Tune-Up Reading

英文を読み、内容に合っていればT、合っていなければFを選びましょう。

CheckLink　DL 03　CD 03

Say hello to Pepper. Pepper is one of the world's first social humanoid robots. He is 120 cm tall, weighs 29 kg and has a curvy design. He costs about ¥200,000. Pepper reads people's emotions by studying their expressions and voice tones. He also remembers facial features and communicates with people in 15 languages through conversation and his touch screen. Pepper does lots of interesting work in many different places.

1. Pepper is one meter tall. 　　　　　　　　　　　　　　　　　T / F
2. Pepper is able to understand people's feelings. 　　　　　　　T / F
3. Pepper knows fifty different languages. 　　　　　　　　　　T / F

11

○ 英語の動詞にはbe動詞と一般動詞の2種類があります。

○ be動詞は、主語の状態や様子を説明するときに使います。主語によって形が変わります。

組み合わせ 主語＋be動詞		主語を説明する ことば	意味
I	**am**	a soccer fan.	私はサッカーのファンです。
You	**are**	busy.	あなたは忙しいです。
He / She / It	**is**	popular.	彼／彼女／それは人気があります。
We / You / They	**are**	from Okinawa.	私たち／あなたたち／彼らは沖縄出身です。

[否定文] I **am** [I'm] **not** afraid of ghosts.　私はおばけが怖くありません。

[疑問文] **Is** this book interesting?　この本はおもしろいですか。

○ 一般動詞は、主語の動作・状態・性質を表すときに使います。

主語	一般動詞	その他の情報	意味
I	**have**	an English test today.	今日、私は英語のテストがあります。
You	**play**	the guitar very well.	あなたはギターをとても上手に弾きます。
Emily	**travels**	all over the world.	エミリーは世界中を旅します。
Ken and Meg	**work**	for a real-estate company.	ケンとメグは不動産会社で働いています。

▶主語がI/You以外の単数形で時制が現在の場合、一般動詞の語尾に -s[-es] をつけます。

[否定文] I **don't like** spicy food.　私は辛い食べ物が好きではありません。

John **never forgets** his friends' birthdays.
ジョンは決して友達の誕生日を忘れません。

[疑問文] **Do** you **listen** to classical music?　あなたはクラシック音楽を聞きますか。

[命令文] **Clean** your room every day.　あなたの部屋を毎日掃除しなさい。

Grammar Hunt!

| Tune-Up Reading | の英文をもう一度読み、be動詞と一般動詞の現在形を探して、be動詞には一重線を、一般動詞には二重線を引きましょう。be動詞は<u>2箇所</u>、一般動詞は<u>8箇所</u>あります。

Grammar Practice

A (   ) 内から正しい選択肢を選び、文を完成させましょう。　◯CheckLink

1. (**a.** Are **b.** Do **c.** Is) Jim and Linda from the United States?
2. The train (**a.** leave **b.** leaves **c.** is leave) from Platform 10.
3. I (**a.** am not **b.** doesn't **c.** don't) have classes on Saturdays.
4. (**a.** Please you open **b.** Please open **c.** You are please open) the window.
5. This book (**a.** doesn't **b.** hasn't **c.** isn't) very interesting.
6. (**a.** Does it **b.** It's **c.** Is it) snow here in winter?
7. Paul never (**a.** is watch **b.** doesn't watch **c.** watches) TV.
8. Do these bananas (**a.** are from **b.** come from **c.** from) the Philippines?

B 日本語に合う文を作りましょう。

1. 彼は大学生です。

_____

2. あなたは東京に住んでいますか。

_____

Prepare to Read

空所に入る適当な語句を選び、1〜5の表現を完成させましょう。その後、音声を聞いて答えを確認しましょう。　◯CheckLink　🎧 DL 04　◎ CD 04

1. お客を案内する　　　　_____ customers
2. お年寄りの世話をする　_____ older people
3. 訪問者と交流する　　　_____ with visitors
4. 家族とつながる　　　　_____ with family members
5. クセを学習する　　　　_____ your habits

| connect | guide | learn | interact | take care of |

Enjoy Reading

A 英文を読みましょう。Q1〜3の質問の答えとなる部分には<u>下線</u>を引きましょう。

DL 05 〜 07　　CD 05 〜 CD 07

Pepper is a collaboration between the robotics company SoftBank Robotics and SoftBank Corp. SoftBank uses the robot to welcome and guide customers at many of its stores throughout Japan.

5　　We also see Pepper as a crew member on ocean cruises, in supermarkets, hotels, restaurants, hospitals and offices. He is available as a research and educational robot for schools and universities. He helps take care of older people in care homes. Pepper also works at the Smithsonian in Washington, D.C.
10　He interacts with visitors, gives them information and plays games with children. He even has his own security badge!

Pepper is also a welcome addition to many homes. He is very kind-hearted and friendly, and his voice and touch are almost human. He loves to connect with family members.
15　He learns your habits, your likes and dislikes, and so on. Downloadable software also allows you to personalize him according to your wants and needs. He laughs and jokes and has real-life conversations. Now don't you want a Pepper robot of your own?

Q1

ペッパーは
ソフトバンクの
店舗で何をして
いる?

Q2

ペッパーはどん
な場所で働い
ている?

Q3

ペッパーが大好
きなことは?

Notes　the Smithsonian「スミソニアン博物館」　security badge「社員証、ID」　and so on「〜など」
personalize「個人向けに設定する」

B 英文の内容についてまとめましょう。下から適切な語句を選んで空所に書き込み、サマリーチャートを完成させましょう。 ⟲ CheckLink

ペッパーの開発

Pepper was created through a ¹( ) between SoftBank Robotics and SoftBank Corp.

さまざまな場所で活躍するペッパー

▶ Schools and universities ➡ He works as a ²( ) and educational robot.

▶ Care homes ➡ He helps ³( ) older people.

▶ The Smithsonian ➡ He ⁴( ) with visitors.

家庭でのペッパーの役割

▶ Pepper learns family members' ⁵( ), likes and dislikes.

▶ Pepper has real-life ⁶( ) with family members.

research	habits	collaboration
interacts	conversations	take care of

C 英文の内容を正しく述べている文になるよう、適切な語句を選びましょう。 ⟲ CheckLink

1. The Smithsonian is in (**a.** Seattle, Washington **b.** Washington, D.C. **c.** New York).

2. Pepper (**a.** gives information **b.** sells tickets **c.** cleans floors) at the Smithsonian.

3. It is possible to personalize Pepper by (**a.** taking him to a SoftBank shop **b.** ordering extra parts **c.** downloading software).

Word Collector

A （　　）内のアルファベットを並べ替え、イラストに合う単語を完成させましょう。

❶ （ yese ）

_ _ _ _

❷ （ eyeswrob ）

eye_ _ _ _ _

❸ （ seno ）

_ _ _ _

❹ （ rase ）

_ _ _ _

❺ （ hotmu ）

_ _ _ _ _

❻ （ tethe ）

_ _ _ _ _

❼ （ breda ）

b_ _ _ _

❽ （ musthace ）

must_ _ _ _

B 日本語に合う文を完成させましょう。（　　）には動詞、下線部には **A** で学んだ語句が入ります。

1. 私たちは目で見て耳で聞きます。

We （　　　　　） with our _____ and （　　　　　） with our _____.

2. 私の祖父は口髭と長いあごひげを生やしています。

My grandfather （　　　　　） a _____ and a long _____.

What's It Like to Be a Self-Sufficient Family?

代名詞

Words to Pictures

次のイラストに合う単語をa～dから選びましょう。 CheckLink DL 08 CD 08

1. (　　)   **2.** (　　)   **3.** (　　)   **4.** (　　)

| **a.** electricity | **b.** farm | **c.** furniture | **d.** sheep |

Tune-Up Reading

英文を読み、内容に合っていればT、合っていなければFを選びましょう。

 CheckLink DL 09 CD 09

Some towns and villages in the United States, Canada and other countries are self-sufficient. Families eat foods that they produce themselves in their gardens or on their farms. They raise cows, pigs, sheep and chickens, and make their own clothes and furniture. The families have no electricity or other modern technologies or conveniences. It's a happy, quiet and peaceful life for them. Does this kind of life interest you?

Notes   self-sufficient「自給自足の」 conveniences「文明の利器」

1. There are self-sufficient communities only in the U.S and Canada.   T / F
2. All of the families are vegetarian.   T / F
3. The families don't own any furniture.   T / F

Grammar Basics

⭕ 代名詞は、前に出てきた名詞を言い換えるときなどに使います。

This is <u>Tom</u>. **He** is from Canada.
こちらはトムです。彼はカナダから来ました。

<u>Nancy and Beth</u> go to the same school.
They are classmates.
ナンシーとベスは同じ学校に通っています。
彼女たちはクラスメイトです。

⭕ 代名詞の格変化：文中での働きによって形が変わります。

主格 「〜は／〜が」 主語になる	所有格 「〜の」 後ろには名詞が来る	目的格 「〜を」 目的語になる 前置詞の後に来る	所有代名詞 「〜のもの」	再帰代名詞 「〜自身」 「〜自身で」
I	my	me	mine	myself
you	your	you	yours	yourself yourselves
he	his	him	his	himself
she	her	her	hers	herself
it	its	it	–	itself
we	our	us	ours	ourselves
they	their	them	theirs	themselves

⭕ 所有代名詞（〜のもの）は、後ろに名詞を置かずに単体で使います。

Please give me your <u>phone number</u>. I'll give you **mine**.
あなたの電話番号を教えてください。私のもの（電話番号）もあなたに教えます。

This isn't <u>Patty's bicycle</u>. **Hers** has a red saddle.
これはパティの自転車ではありません。彼女のもの（自転車）には赤いサドルがついています。

⭕ 主語と目的語が同じものを指しているとき、再帰代名詞を使います。

<u>We</u> enjoyed **ourselves** at the party. 私たちはパーティを楽しみました。

<u>Jim</u> saw **himself** in the mirror. ジムは鏡に映る自分自身を見ました。

Grammar Hunt!

Tune-Up Reading の英文をもう一度読み、代名詞を探して下線を引きましょう。下線は9箇所あります。

Grammar Practice

A （　　）内から正しい選択肢を選び、文を完成させましょう。　⟳CheckLink

1. (**a.** Their **b.** They **c.** Them) have soccer practice every day after school.
2. (**a.** He **b.** Him **c.** His) hobby is building plastic models.
3. Jim's children are over there. Do you see (**a.** it **b.** him **c.** them)?
4. This herb tea helps (**a.** I **b.** me **c.** my) to relax.
5. Is this (**a.** your **b.** yours **c.** you're) pen?
6. Those suitcases are (**a.** their **b.** theirs **c.** themselves).
7. The company sells (**a.** its **b.** they **c.** theirs) products all over the world.
8. Margaret makes (**a.** herself **b.** himself **c.** ourselves) a cup of tea every night.

B （　　）内に適切な代名詞を入れて、文を完成させましょう。

1. Harry has a new car. (　　　　　　　　) is a Toyota.
2. Mary always does (　　　　　　) homework after school.
3. I don't like green peas. I never eat (　　　　　　).
4. This isn't my coat. (　　　　　　) is brown.

Prepare to Read

空所に入る適当な単語を選び、1〜5の表現を完成させましょう。その後、音声を聞いて答えを確認しましょう。　⟳CheckLink　🎧 DL 10　◎ CD 10

1. 子どもたちを起こす　　　＿＿＿＿＿＿＿＿ up the children
2. 洋服を干す　　　　　　　＿＿＿＿＿＿＿＿ clothes
3. 家畜に餌をやる　　　　　＿＿＿＿＿＿＿＿ the farm animals
4. 馬と馬車　　　　　　horse and ＿＿＿＿＿＿＿
5. 家事　　　　　　　　household ＿＿＿＿＿＿＿

feed	hang	buggy	chores	wake

19

Enjoy Reading

A 英文を読みましょう。Ｑ１〜３の質問の答えとなる部分には<u>下線</u>を引きましょう。

🎧 DL 11 ~ 13　◎ CD 11 ~ ◎ CD 13

A day in the life of a typical self-sufficient family starts with the ringing of an alarm clock. Mother wakes up her six children, and then makes breakfast and school lunches for them. She does laundry with an old-fashioned washing machine. She hangs the plain and simple clothes on a long laundry rope.

5

Father goes to the barn to take care of his horses and to feed the other farm animals. The family's "car" is a horse and buggy. They use horses to plow the field. Everyone in the family does household chores or works on the farm. To earn money, they sell their organic vegetables and handicrafts at a roadside stand or farmers market, or to restaurants in nearby towns.

10

The children go to school for eight years. Their parents also teach them at night. But life is not all hard work for them. They enjoy activities such as card games, board games, reading, fishing, camping and sports. Some of their neighbors have Internet and smartphones, but this family continues to live just as their ancestors did 300 years ago. They like it that way.

15

20

Q1

自給自足の家族の1日は何から始まる？

Q2

家族は車の代わりに何を使っている？

Q3

子どもたちはどんなことを楽しんでいる？

Notes　barn「納屋」　plow「耕す」　handicrafts「工芸品」　roadside stand「道路沿いの売店」
neighbors「ご近所に住む人」　ancestors「祖先」

B 英文の内容についてまとめましょう。下から適切な語句を選んで空所に書き込み、サマリーチャートを完成させましょう。　*CheckLink*

母親の仕事

▶ Mother wakes up her children, and makes ¹(   ) and ²(   ) for them.

▶ She uses an old-fashioned washing machine to do ³(   ).

父親と家族の仕事

▶ Father takes care of the horses and feeds the other farm animals.

▶ The family members do ⁴(   ) or work on the farm.

▶ They sell their organic vegetables and ⁵(   ).

子供たちの生活

▶ They study not only at school but also at home with the help of their ⁶(   ).

▶ They also enjoy games, reading, fishing, camping and sports.

| laundry | school lunches | handicrafts |
| household chores | parents | breakfast |

C 英文の内容を正しく述べている文になるよう、適切な語句を選びましょう。　*CheckLink*

1. The family uses (**a.** hand tools **b.** horses **c.** machines) to plow the field.

2. The children attend school for (**a.** 6 **b.** 8 **c.** 12) years.

3. This family doesn't have any (**a.** simple tools **b.** neighbors **c.** modern conveniences).

Hobbies and Games

A 日本語をヒントに、動詞の後に続く名詞をa〜hから選びましょう。

❶ 切手を集める　　　collect ＿＿＿

❷ スケッチをする　　draw ＿＿＿

❸ ハイキングに行く　go ＿＿＿

❹ セーターを編む　　knit ＿＿＿

❺ 陶器を作る　　　　make ＿＿＿

❻ トランプをする　　play ＿＿＿

❼ マンガを読む　　　read ＿＿＿

❽ 写真を撮る　　　　take ＿＿＿

> **a.** cards
> **b.** photographs
> **c.** sketches
> **d.** sweaters
> **e.** stamps
> **f.** hiking
> **g.** comics
> **h.** pottery

B 日本語に合う文を完成させましょう。（　　）には代名詞、下線部には **A** で学んだ語句が入ります。

1. ベンは切手を集めます。彼は2,000以上のコレクションを持っています。

Ben ＿＿＿＿＿＿＿＿＿＿＿＿＿. (　　　　) has more than 2,000 in (　　　　)

collection.

2. メアリーと弟は空き時間にトランプをして遊びます。

Mary and (　　　　) brother ＿＿＿＿＿＿＿＿＿＿ in (　　　　) free time.

Why Did Starbucks Become a Hit in Japan?

過去形

Words to Pictures

次のイラストに合う語句をa〜dから選びましょう。　CheckLink　DL 14　CD 14

1. (　　)　　　　**2.** (　　)　　　　**3.** (　　)　　　　**4.** (　　)

a. graduate from university　　**c.** sell equipment
b. open a shop　　　　　　　　**d.** start a career

Tune-Up Reading

英文を読み、内容に合っていればT、合っていなければFを選びましょう。

CheckLink　DL 15　CD 15

Three friends, Jerry Baldwin, Zev Siegl and Gordon Bowker, graduated from the University of San Francisco and started their own careers.　One thing later brought them together again — their love of coffee.　In 1971, they opened their first Starbucks coffee shop in Seattle, Washington.　At first, they sold only high-quality coffee beans and coffee-making equipment.　Starbucks now has around 30,000 shops in more than 75 countries, including Japan.

1. Jerry Baldwin, Zev Siegl and Gordon Bowker attended the same university.

T / F

2. The three men made their own coffee-making equipment.　　　　T / F
3. The first Starbucks coffee shop opened in Washington, D.C.　　　T / F

23

Grammar Basics

○ 過去に起こったことを言うときは、動詞を過去形にします。

○ be動詞の過去形は was / were を使って表します。

組み合わせ 主語＋be動詞		主語を説明することば	意味
I	was	at home last night.	私は昨夜、家にいました。
You	were	late for class this morning.	あなたは今朝、授業に遅刻しました。
The weather (He / She / It)	was	very good yesterday.	昨日はお天気がとてもよかったです。
Jeff and I (We / You / They)	were	roommates in college.	ジェフと私は大学時代にルームメイトでした。

[否定文] Tom **was not [wasn't]** at the party.　トムはパーティにはいませんでした。

[疑問文] **Were** you hungry at that time?　そのときあなたはお腹がすいていましたか。

○ 一般動詞の過去形には、規則変化するものと不規則変化するものがあります。

	主語	一般動詞	その他の情報	意味
規則変化	I	cooked	dinner for my parents.	私は両親のために夕食を作りました。
	You	asked	many questions.	あなたはたくさん質問しました。
不規則変化	We	had	an important meeting yesterday.	私たちは昨日、重要な会議がありました。
	Emma	lost	her key.	エマは自分の鍵をなくしました。

[否定文]　I **didn't know** about the news.　私はそのニュースについて知りませんでした。
　　　　　They **did not [didn't] go** to the stadium.　彼らはスタジアムに行きませんでした。

[疑問文]　**Did** you **go** to school yesterday?　あなたは昨日学校に行きましたか。
　　　　　Did Bob **study** economics at college?　ボブは大学で経済学を勉強しましたか。

Grammar Hunt!

Tune-Up Reading の英文をもう一度読み、一般動詞の過去形を探して下線を引きましょう。下線は５箇所あります。

Grammar Practice

A （　）内から正しい選択肢を選び、文を完成させましょう。　⟳CheckLink

1. Henry (**a.** came **b.** come **c.** was came) to Japan six years ago.
2. (**a.** Did **b.** Was **c.** Were) you tired last night?
3. Janet (**a.** had **b.** was have **c.** has) a car accident yesterday.
4. Fred (**a.** aren't went **b.** didn't go **c.** didn't went) to class today.
5. This computer (**a.** cost **b.** was cost **c.** was costing) only $200.
6. (**a.** Are you studied **b.** Did you studied **c.** Did you study) for the test?
7. No one (**a.** knew **b.** didn't know **c.** was knowing) the answer to the question.
8. (**a.** Was Susan run **b.** Did Susan run **c.** Did run Susan) in the marathon?

B 日本語に合う文を作りましょう。

1. 彼女は自分のスマートフォンをなくしました。

_____

2. あなたは昨日銀行に行きましたか。

_____

Prepare to Read

空所に入る適当な単語を選び、1〜5の表現を完成させましょう。その後、音声を聞いて答えを確認しましょう。　⟳CheckLink　⬇ DL 16　◎ CD 16

1. 飲み物のオプションを提供する　_____ drink options
2. コーヒーを飲まない人を魅了する　_____ non-coffee drinkers
3. 禁煙環境を導入する　_____ a smoke-free environment
4. 心地よい雰囲気を楽しむ　_____ a pleasant atmosphere
5. 見た目を変える　_____ the appearance

| attract | enjoy | change | offer | introduce |

Enjoy Reading

A 英文を読みましょう。Q1～3の質問の答えとなる部分には<u>下線を引きましょう。</u>

🎧 DL 17 ~ 19　◎CD 17 ~ ◎CD 19

The great success story of Starbucks Japan began in 1996.
Starbucks was the first coffee shop to offer drink options such
as soy milk latte. In addition, it attracted many non-coffee
drinkers with its Frappuccinos. Starbucks also became the
5　first coffee shop chain to introduce a smoke-free environment
in all of its shops. This appealed to a lot of young people,
including couples with small children. Starbucks also added
drive-throughs at some of its locations.

Starbucks knew that customers come not only to drink
10　coffee, but also to enjoy a pleasant atmosphere. The coffee
shop follows trends and sometimes changes the appearance
of its stores to make them look like trendy American cafés.

Another big step that Starbucks took was to learn about
Japanese culture. It began selling seasonal drinks such as
15　Sakura (cherry blossom) Frappuccino and Hojicha Tea Latte.
Starbucks also built concept stores in historical areas. For
example, the store in front of Izumo Grand Shrine (Izumo
Taisha) has a Japanese style design. The store's atmosphere
goes well with the view of the shrine.

Q1

日本にスター
バックスが上陸
したのは何年？

Q2

客はコーヒー以
外に何を求めて
スターバックス
に来る？

Q3

日本ならでは
のスターバック
スのドリンクメ
ニューは？

B 英文の内容についてまとめましょう。下から適切な語句を選んで空所に書き込み、サマリーチャートを完成させましょう。 ↻**CheckLink**

さまざまな「日本発」

Starbucks Japan was the first coffee shop chain to...

① offer drinks such as ¹( ) and Frappuccinos.

② introduce a ²( ) environment.

お店の雰囲気づくり

▶ Some of the stores ³( ) like trendy
⁴( ).

日本ならではのスターバックス

▶ Starbucks started selling ⁵( ).

▶ They also built concept stores in historical areas such as
⁶( ).

| American cafés | smoke-free | Izumo Grand Shrine |
| look | seasonal drinks | soy milk latte |

C 英文の内容を正しく述べている文になるよう、適切な語句を選びましょう。 ↻**CheckLink**

1. Starbucks attracted non-coffee drinkers with its (**a.** sparkling water
b. non-alcohol beer **c.** Frappuccinos).

2. Couples with young children liked the (**a.** no-smoking rule **b.** play areas for
children **c.** drive-throughs).

3. Starbucks learned about Japanese (**a.** climate **b.** culture **c.** companies).

Word Pairs

A もっともよく一緒に使われる単語の組み合わせを完成させましょう。

❶ bread & _____

❷ cream & _____

❸ curry & _____

❹ hot & _____

❺ oil & _____

❻ salt & _____

| pepper | butter | sugar | rice | spicy | vinegar |

B 以下は、昨夜のエミリーの夕飯に関する文です。 ▢ には（　　）内の動詞の過去形を入れ、下線部には **A** で学んだ語句を使用して文を完成させましょう。

Emily _____ (eat) _____ for dinner last night.

It _____ (be) very _____!

How Do Americans Celebrate Halloween?

可算名詞・不可算名詞

Words to Pictures

次のイラストに合う単語を a〜d から選びましょう。　CheckLink　DL 20　CD 20

1. (　　) **2.** (　　) **3.** (　　) **4.** (　　)

a. costume　　**b.** shout　　**c.** treat　　**d.** trick-or-treating

Tune-Up Reading

英文を読み、内容に合っていれば T、合っていなければ F を選びましょう。

CheckLink　DL 21　CD 21

What day is October 31? That's right — it's Halloween. In the US, trick-or-treating is part of the Halloween fun. Children dress up in costumes, knock on neighbors' doors and shout "Trick or treat!" They usually receive a treat such as chocolate, or sometimes money. No treat? Then it's time to play a trick, like knocking again later and then running away. Many American teenagers and adults celebrate Halloween, too.

1. Halloween is on the last day of October.　　　　　　T / F
2. Children usually receive money as a treat.　　　　　　T / F
3. In the United States, only children celebrate Halloween.　　T / F

Grammar Basics

○ 英語には数えられる名詞と数えられない名詞があります。数えられる名詞は単数形と複数形を区別します。

○ 数えられる名詞（可算名詞）には複数形があります。

語尾に -s/-esをつける	egg – eggs / photo – photos / speech – speeches
語尾を変えて-esをつける	story – stories / leaf – leaves
不規則変化する	man-men / child-children / foot-feet

○ 数えられない名詞（不可算名詞）には複数形がないので、しばしば数量を表す語句と一緒に使います。

物質名詞	chocolate（チョコレート）、meat（肉）、money（お金）、rain（雨）、salt（塩）、silver（銀）、water（水） ▶ **some** money / **a bar of** chocolate / **a drop of** water など
抽象名詞	advice（助言）、fun（楽しみ）、information（情報）、news（ニュース）、time（時間） ※回数を表すtimeは可算名詞 ▶ **a lot of** fun / **a piece of** information / **plenty of** time など
集合名詞	baggage/luggage（手荷物）、equipment（設備）、furniture（家具類）、fruit（果実）、machinery（機械類）、jewelry（宝飾品） ▶ **a piece** of furniture など

○ many/a few/fewは可算名詞に、much/a little/littleは不可算名詞と一緒に使います。some/anyは両方のタイプの名詞と一緒に使うことができます。

I spent **a few hours** at a café in front of the station.
私は駅前のカフェで数時間過ごしました。

The man had **little money** with him.
その男はほとんどお金を持っていませんでした。

I didn't buy **any** souvenirs.
私はおみやげを何も買いませんでした。

▶anyは否定文と疑問文、someは肯定文に使います。

Grammar Hunt! | Tune-Up Reading | の英文をもう一度読み、数えられる名詞の複数形を探して下線を引きましょう。下線は6箇所あります。

Grammar Practice

A (　　) 内から正しい選択肢を選び、文を完成させましょう。　 CheckLink

1. Takeshi eats (**a.** a rice **b.** rice **c.** rices) for breakfast every morning.
2. There aren't (**a.** an egg **b.** some eggs **c.** any eggs) in the refrigerator.
3. It snowed (**a.** any **b.** many **c.** much) times last winter.
4. I slept only (**a.** a few **b.** few **c.** a little) hours last night.
5. Wendy usually listens to (**a.** a music **b.** music **c.** some musics) on the train.
6. Did you finish your (**a.** homework **b.** homeworks **c.** a homework)?
7. Jerry doesn't eat (**a.** little **b.** much **c.** few) meat.
8. This museum has many wonderful (**a.** art **b.** picture **c.** paintings).

B (　　) 内に a / an / some のいずれかを入れて、文を完成させましょう。

1. Do you have (　　　　　　　) part-time job?
2. Ellen took (　　　　　　　) photos of Mt. Fuji.
3. He gave (　　　　　　　) interesting speech.
4. Let's buy (　　　　　　　) fruit at the market.

Prepare to Read

空所に入る適当な語句を選び、1〜5の表現を完成させましょう。その後、音声を聞いて答えを確認しましょう。　 CheckLink　 DL 22　 CD 22

1. お化け屋敷を訪れる　　　　　_____ haunted houses
2. 飾りつけをする　　　　　　　_____ decorations
3. ハロウィーンの仮装パーティに出席する

　　　　　　　　　　　　　　　_____ Halloween costume parties
4. 地域で行われる　　　　　　　_____ the neighborhood
5. 仮装姿で現れる　　　　　　　_____ in costumes

| attend | take place in | put up | show up | visit |

31

A 英文を読みましょう。Q１〜３の質問の答えとなる部分には<u>下線を引きましょう</u>。

DL 23 ~ 25　　CD 23　~　CD 25

Every year, about 90 percent of American children go trick-or-treating on Halloween night. Young adults like to have fun on Halloween, too. Many people watch scary movies, visit haunted houses, or enjoy ghost stories. People
5　also like to send Halloween cards and put up decorations. About two-thirds of adults between the ages of 18 and 34 attend Halloween costume parties or other celebrations such as parades.

The largest Halloween parade in the world is the Village
10　Halloween Parade. It takes place in the Greenwich Village neighborhood of New York City. It's the city's only nighttime parade. Every year on October 31, around 50,000 "night creatures" show up in costumes. Another two million people come to watch.

15　Greenwich Village puppeteer and mask maker Ralph Lee began the event in 1973. The parade is famous for its hundreds of amazing four-meter-tall puppets. In addition to the puppets, dozens of bands, dancers, artists and Halloween parade floats participate each year. The parade usually goes
20　from 7 to 10:30 p.m. along a 2.25-kilometer route.

Notes　puppeteer「人形使い」　floats「山車（だし）」

Q1

アメリカの子どもたちの何％がトリック・オア・トリートに出かける？

Q2

世界最大級のハロウィーンパレードの名前は？

Q3

パレードが始まったのはいつで、誰が始めた？

32

B 英文の内容についてまとめましょう。下から適切な語句を選んで空所に書き込み、サマリーチャートを完成させましょう。 CheckLink

アメリカの人たちがハロウィーンにすること

▶ go ¹( ) ➡ 主に子ども

▶ enjoy ²( ) movies, haunted houses, or ghost stories

▶ send Halloween cards and put up ³( )

▶ attend Halloween parties and parades

世界最大級のハロウィーンパレード

▶ The Village Halloween Parade ⁴( ) in New York City.

▶ People in costumes show up as "⁵( )."

パレードの様子

▶ We can see hundreds of four-meter-tall ⁶( ), and many bands, dancers, artists and floats.

night creatures	trick-or-treating	decorations
takes place	scary	puppets

C 英文の内容を正しく述べている文になるよう、適切な語句を選びましょう。 CheckLink

1. About (**a.** 50% **b.** 65% **c.** 90%) of young American adults celebrate Halloween.

2. Every year, (**a.** 20,000 **b.** 200,000 **c.** 2,000,000) people watch the Village Halloween Parade.

3. The Halloween parade is usually (**a.** 2.5 **b.** 3 **c.** 3.5) hours long.

33

Word Collector

Halloween Costumes

A ①〜⑧はハロウィーンのコスチュームです。イラストに合う単語を選びましょう。

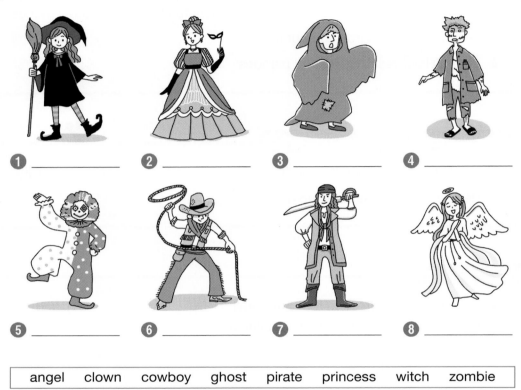

① _____

② _____

③ _____

④ _____

⑤ _____

⑥ _____

⑦ _____

⑧ _____

| angel | clown | cowboy | ghost | pirate | princess | witch | zombie |

B 以下の文には誤りがあります。イラストについて正しく描写する文になるよう、誤りを正して書き直しましょう。

The clown has two flowers on his hats, curly hairs and big nose. He has a lot of make-up on his faces. He has big shoe.

_____

_____

_____

Do You Want to Travel Back in Time to a Roman *Thermae*?

時と場所を表す前置詞

Words to Pictures

次のイラストに合う語句をa～dから選びましょう。　 CheckLink　 DL 26　 CD 26

1. (　　) 　　　　**2.** (　　) 　　　　**3.** (　　) 　　　　**4.** (　　)

a. ancient Rome 　　**b.** modern-day Japan 　　**c.** public bath 　　**d.** time travel

Tune-Up Reading

英文を読み、内容に合っていればT、合っていなければFを選びましょう。

CheckLink　 DL 27　 CD 27

Thermae Romae was a hit Japanese movie in 2012.　The main character, Lucius, designs public baths (*thermae*) in ancient Rome.　However, his designs are old-fashioned, and he loses his job.　One day, Lucius visits a *thermae* and accidentally travels through time to modern-day Japan.　During his time travel, he discovers Japanese bath culture.　He returns to Rome, and everyone loves his futuristic Japanese *thermae* designs.　But what were Roman *thermae* really like?

Note　 accidentally「偶然に」

1. *Thermae* means "hot water." 　　　　　　　　　　　　　　　　　　T / F
2. Lucius designed a time machine. 　　　　　　　　　　　　　　　　　T / F
3. Lucius designed modern and unique *thermae* after his time travel. 　T / F

35

○ 前置詞は、後ろに名詞を伴って時や場所を表します。以下は時を表す前置詞です。

ある時点／時期に・で	
at（時間、時点） **on**（日付、曜日） **in**（午前・午後、月、年など）	Please call me **at** eight o'clock tonight. 今晩8時に私に電話してください。 I often play the piano **in** the evening. 私はよく夕方にピアノを弾きます。
〜の間に、〜の間ずっと	
for（時間の長さ） **during**（期間） **through**（特定の期間）	We stayed in Okinawa **for** a month last summer. 私たちは去年の夏、沖縄に1ヵ月滞在しました。 My brother sleeps **during** the day and works **at** night. 私の兄（弟）は昼間は寝ていて、夜に働いています。
〜まで	
until（期限までずっと） **by**（期限までに）	I studied at the library **until** ten o'clock last night. 私は昨晩、10時まで図書館で勉強していました。 Please come back here **by** four o'clock. 4時までにはここに戻ってきてください。

○ 以下は場所を表す前置詞です。

in（〜の中に・で） **into**（〜の中へ）	Please wait **in** this room until he comes. 彼が来るまでこの部屋の中で待っていてください。 The children went **into** the museum. その子どもたちは美術館の中へ入っていきました。
next to（〜の隣に・で）	I usually sit **next to** Lisa in English class. 私は英語の授業のときはたいていリサの隣に座ります。
near（〜の近くに・で）	A new supermarket opened **near** my house. 新しいスーパーが私の家の近くにオープンしました。
on（〜の上に・で）	Your key is **on** the table. あなたの鍵はテーブルの上にあります。
under（〜の下に・で）	A cat is sleeping **under** the sofa. ソファーの下で猫が眠っています。

Grammar Hunt!

Tune-Up Reading の英文をもう一度読み、このページで学んだ時と場所を表す前置詞を探して下線を引きましょう。下線は4箇所あります。

Grammar Practice

A （　　）内から正しい選択肢を選び、文を完成させましょう。　　⟳CheckLink

1. Ken exercises (**a.** for　**b.** in　**c.** at) 30 minutes every day.

2. The jazz festival is (**a.** at　**b.** in　**c.** on) Saturday and Sunday.

3. Bruce fell asleep (**a.** by　**b.** during　**c.** for) the test.

4. The last train leaves (**a.** at　**b.** on　**c.** to) midnight.

5. She left her cellphone (**a.** at　**b.** in　**c.** on) the classroom.

6. Cathy sits (**a.** into　**b.** under　**c.** next to) Jennifer in math class.

7. There's a nice restaurant (**a.** through　**b.** near　**c.** on) the park.

8. This department store sells kitchen goods (**a.** at　**b.** in　**c.** on) the 5th floor.

B 日本語に合う文を作りましょう。

1. コンサートは午後7時に始まります。

_____

2. チケットは新聞の下にありました。

_____

Prepare to Read

空所に入る適当な単語を選び、1〜5の表現を完成させましょう。その後、音声を聞いて答えを確認しましょう。　　⟳CheckLink　🎧 DL 28　◎ CD 28

1. 紀元前1世紀　　　　　　the first _____ BC

2. 人工の温泉　　　　　　_____ hot springs

3. ローマ帝国　　　　　　the Roman _____

4. 熱風風呂　　　　　　　_____ bath

5. 政治について議論する　discuss _____

| politics | hot-air | century | Empire | artificial |

A 英文を読みましょう。Q１～３の質問の答えとなる部分には<u>下線を引きましょう。</u>

DL 29 ~ 31　◎ CD 29 ~ ◎ CD 31

A rich Roman businessman got the idea for *thermae* at the beginning of the first century BC. He knew that there were some natural hot springs near Mt. Vesuvius. He created artificial hot springs by heating water with log fires under
5　buildings. These small bath houses, or *balnea*, were very popular, and soon the Roman Empire started building huge public bath houses, or *thermae*.

Many Romans bathed for several hours each day in different kinds of baths. In general, after paying a small
10　fee, visitors took off their clothes in the changing room and then exercised in the sports hall. Next, they entered the cold bath or cooled down in the swimming pool. From there, they moved to the warm bath or went directly into the hot bath. After that, they took a hot-air bath.

15　Bathing was an important part of Roman life and culture. But visitors didn't visit *thermae* only to take a bath. In addition to sports areas, *thermae* also had parks, restaurants, and sometimes libraries and small theaters. People chatted with friends and strangers, and often
20　discussed politics or business.

Notes　Mt. Vesuvius「ヴェスヴィオ火山」　log fires「暖炉、焚き火」　bathe「入浴する」

Q1

テルマエのアイディアを考えたのは誰？

Q2

ローマ人たちは１日どのくらいの時間、浴場にいた？

Q3

ローマ人にとって入浴とはどのようなものだった？

B 英文の内容についてまとめましょう。下から適切な語句を選んで空所に書き込み、サマリーチャートを完成させましょう。 ↻CheckLink

テルマエ誕生のきっかけ

▶ There were some ¹( ) hot springs near Mt. Vesuvius.

▶ A rich Roman businessman created small bath houses with ²( ) hot springs. ➡ その後、ローマ帝国でテルマエが作られ始めた

ローマ人の公共浴場での過ごし方

Step 1	Visitors paid an entrance fee.
Step 2	They took off their clothes and ³( ) in the sports hall.
Step 3	They entered the ⁴( ) bath or the swimming pool.
Step 4	They moved to the warm bath or went into the ⁵( ) bath.
Step 5	They took a hot-air bath.

テルマエ＝ローマ人の生活にかかせない存在

▶ *Thermae* also had parks, restaurants, libraries and small theaters.

▶ People talked with friends and ⁶( ), and often discussed politics or business.

hot	cold	natural
artificial	exercised	strangers

C 英文の内容を正しく述べている文になるよう、適切な語句を選びましょう。 ↻CheckLink

1. The Romans began building *thermae* more than (**a.** 1,000 **b.** 2,000 **c.** 3,000) years ago.

2. *Balnea* means (**a.** hot water **b.** hot springs **c.** small bath houses).

3. The Roman baths were (**a.** inexpensive **b.** expensive **c.** free of charge).

Bathhouse Etiquette

A 次のクロスワードパズルを完成させましょう。

Across

1. We dry ourselves with a _____.
2. We use a hair _____ to dry our hair.
3. We wash our hair with _____.
4. Some people curl their hair with a curling _____.

Down

5. We shave with a _____.
6. We use a _____ to brush our teeth.
7. We rinse our hair under the _____.
8. We use _____ to wash our hands and body.

B 1〜4は銭湯でのルールに関する文です。（　）に入る前置詞を選び、文を完成させましょう。

1. Wash your body (　　　　　　) the bath, not in it.
2. Don't eat food (　　　　　　) your bath.
3. Don't wrap a towel (　　　　　　) your body in the bathtub.
4. Wipe your body with a towel (　　　　　　) re-entering the changing room.

| around | before | during | outside |

Are You Going Cashless?

進行形

Words to Pictures

次のイラストに合う語句をa〜dから選びましょう。　CheckLink　DL 32　CD 32

1. (　　)　　　**2.** (　　)　　　**3.** (　　)　　　**4.** (　　)

a. credit card　　**b.** prepaid card　　**c.** QR code　　**d.** mobile wallet

Tune-Up Reading

英文を読み、内容に合っていればT、合っていなければFを選びましょう。

CheckLink　DL 33　CD 33

Today, cashless payment is becoming the standard in many countries. Credit cards and prepaid cards are popular payment options. More recently, people are using QR (Quick Response) codes and making e-money purchases with their mobile wallets. South Korea is leading the way in cashless payment, with a rate of over 95%. On the other hand, Japan's rate is only around 20%. Why is Japan falling behind most other advanced countries?

1. QR means Quick Reply.　　　　　　　　　　　　　　　　　　　　T / F
2. South Korea has a cashless payment rate of over 95%.　　　T / F
3. Japan's cashless payment rate is very high.　　　　　　　　　T / F

○ 現在あるいは過去のある時点で進行中の動作を表す場合や、習慣的に繰り返し行っ ていること（いたこと）を表す場合、進行形を使います。

○ 現在進行形と過去進行形

現在進行形	I **am texting** my friend. 私は友達にメールを送っています。
	John **is having** breakfast with his father now. ジョンは今、父親と朝食を食べています。
	I **am** always **eating** too much. 私はいつも食べすぎてばかりいます。
過去進行形	I **was watching** TV at ten o'clock last night. 私は昨晩10時にテレビを見ていました。
	We **were having** breakfast at eight o'clock this morning. 私たちは今朝の8時に朝食を食べていました。
	My sister **was** always **asking** my parents questions. 私の妹（姉）はいつも両親に質問ばかりしていました。

[否定文] We **are not working** today. 今日、私たちは働いていません。

[疑問文] **Are you having** a good time at the party?
あなたはパーティを楽しんでいますか。

○ 近い未来の予定を表す現在進行形

We **are leaving** for Rome next week. 私たちは来週ローマに向けて出発します。

○ 間違いやすい進行形

日本語では「〜している」と言う場合でも、英語では進行形で表さないことがあります。

[例] 私はダンとティムのことをよく知っています。

　　○ I know Dan and Tim well.
　　× I am knowing Dan and Tim well.

Grammar Hunt!

Tune-Up Reading の英文をもう一度読み、現在進行形（be動詞＋ 〜ing）を探して下線を引きましょう。下線は5箇所あります。be動詞 が省略されている場合もあります。

Grammar Practice

A (　　　) 内から正しい選択肢を選び、文を完成させましょう。　⟳CheckLink

1. Karen (**a.** does learn　**b.** is learning　**c.** is learned) ballet in Russia.
2. (**a.** Are you enjoy　**b.** Do you enjoy　**c.** Are you enjoying) your classes this year?
3. Jim and Ed are (**a.** money saving　**b.** saved money　**c.** saving money) for a trip.
4. These days, a lot of people (**a.** are shopping　**b.** shopping　**c.** shopped) online.
5. Mark (**a.** doesn't eating　**b.** doesn't eats　**c.** isn't eating) much these days.
6. I was (**a.** taken my dog　**b.** taking my dog　**c.** my dog taking) for a walk then.
7. (**a.** Are　**b.** Was　**c.** Were) you sleeping at 11:00 last night?
8. Sorry, I wasn't (**a.** listening to　**b.** understanding　**c.** believing) your story.

B 日本語に合う文を作りましょう。

1. あなたは今レポートを書いていますか。

_____

2. 私は昨日の夜宿題をしていました。

_____

Prepare to Read

空所に入る適当な単語を選び、1～5の表現を完成させましょう。その後、音声を聞いて答えを確認しましょう。　⟳CheckLink　🎧 DL 34　◉ CD 34

1. 自動販売機　　　　　_____ machine
2. 公共交通機関　　　　public _____
3. 定期券　　　　　　　commuter _____
4. 支払い方法　　　　　_____ of payment
5. 現金払いのみを受け付ける　_____ cash only

| accept | pass | transportation | vending | form |

43

Enjoy Reading

A 英文を読みましょう。Q1～3の質問の答えとなる部分には<u>下線を引きましょう</u>。

🎧 DL 35～37　◎CD 35　～　◎CD 37

Japanese people use credit cards and prepaid cards at shops and vending machines, and for public transportation. In fact, such cashless payments are not new to Japan. People were already paying by credit and using commuter passes as
5　long as 40 or 50 years ago. Nowadays, some supermarkets and electronics stores give reward points for cashless payments. More recently, people are starting to use mobile applications.

Surprisingly, however, cash is still the most popular form of payment in this country. Here, people generally feel safe
10　carrying cash. When they're walking along busy streets or riding crowded buses or trains, they don't worry about losing their wallets. Cash payments are also usually quick, and ATMs are easy to find.

In addition, many smaller shops and restaurants in Japan
15　accept cash only. One popular restaurant search service recently found that only about 50,000 out of 135,000 restaurants were accepting credit card payments. Despite Japan's love for cash, the government is promoting e-money payments, and the trend towards a cashless society is growing.

Q1

日本人はどのような場所でキャッシュレスの支払いをしている?

Q2

日本ではどのような支払い方法が好まれている?

Q3

日本政府は何を推進しようとしている?

B 英文の内容についてまとめましょう。下から適切な語句を選んで空所に書き込み、サマリーチャートを完成させましょう。 ↻CheckLink

日本のキャッシュレス事情

40 or 50 years ago	People were already making ¹( ) payments.
Nowadays	Supermarkets and stores give ²( ) for cashless payments.
More recently	People are starting to pay for things using ³( ).

日本人は現金が好き？

理 由
① People feel ⁴( ) carrying cash.
② Cash payments are usually ⁵( ).
③ It is easy to find ATMs.

今後の展望

The trend towards a cashless ⁶( ) is growing.

| quick | reward points | safe |
| society | mobile applications | cashless |

C 英文の内容を正しく述べている文になるよう、適切な語句を選びましょう。 ↻CheckLink

1. People don't worry about losing their wallets (**a.** in public places **b.** at work **c.** in their home).

2. (**a.** Most **b.** About half **c.** About 40%) of restaurants accept cashless payments.

3. The best title for this passage is: (**a.** *Moving Towards Cash-Based Payments* **b.** *Cashless Payments* **c.** *Mobile Phone Payment Apps*) *in Japan*.

Word Collector

A ❶〜❽はお金にまつわるアイテムです。イラストに合う語句を選びましょう。

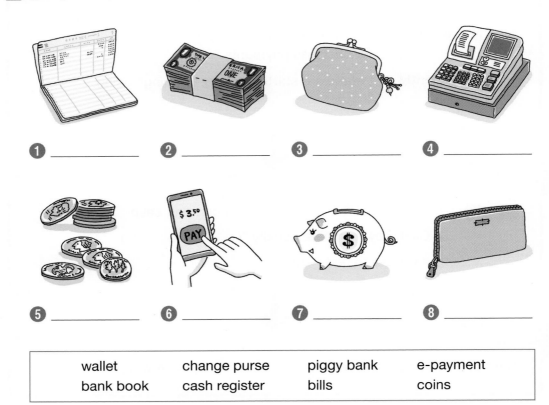

❶ _____

❷ _____

❸ _____

❹ _____

❺ _____

❻ _____

❼ _____

❽ _____

wallet	change purse	piggy bank	e-payment
bank book	cash register	bills	coins

B **A**で学んだ語句を使って、現在進行形を使った文を2つ作りましょう。

1. 彼は新しい財布を買っているところです。

_____

2. ジェーンは昨日通帳を探していました。

_____

Why Are Marathons 42.195 Kilometers Long?

疑問詞

Words to Pictures

次のイラストに合う単語をa～dから選びましょう。　CheckLink　DL 38　CD 38

1. (　　)　　**2.** (　　)　　**3.** (　　)　　**4.** (　　)

a. army　　**b.** messenger　　**c.** marathon　　**d.** soldier

Tune-Up Reading

英文を読み、内容に合っていればT、合っていなければFを選びましょう。

CheckLink　DL 39　CD 39

The first marathon was in Athens, Greece in 1896. How long was the race? It was 40 km long. What was its origin? In 490 BC, a Greek soldier ran about 40 km from Marathon to Athens with news of victory over a Persian army. Soon after delivering the news, the messenger died. His dramatic run gave people the idea for the modern marathon. Then, why aren't marathons 40 km long today?

Notes　Athens, Greece「ギリシャのアテネ」　Marathon「マラトン村」　Persian「ペルシャの」

1. The first marathon ended in Marathon, Greece.　　　　　　　　T　/　F
2. The Greek messenger delivered good news.　　　　　　　　　　T　/　F
3. The messenger ran exactly 42.195 km.　　　　　　　　　　　　T　/　F

○ 疑問詞を使って、「誰／何／いつ／どこ」などの情報をたずねることができます。

Who 誰が・誰を	**Who** do you like in the singing group? その歌手グループの中であなたは誰が好きですか。 **Who** sent you these flowers? 誰があなたに花束を送りましたか。
What 何が・何を	**What** did you buy your brother for his birthday present? あなたはお兄さん（弟）の誕生日プレゼントに何を買いましたか。 **What** surprised you at the party last night? 昨晩のパーティであなたを驚かせたことは何ですか。
When いつ	**When** does the concert start? コンサートはいつ始まりますか。
Where どこで	**Where** are they having the meeting? 彼らはどこで会議をしていますか。
Which どちらの	**Which** picture do you like better? あなたはどちらの絵（写真）が好きですか。 **Which** artist won the award? どちらのアーティストが賞をとりましたか。
Why なぜ	**Why** were you late for class? なぜあなたは授業に遅れたのですか。
How どのように・どのくらい	**How** did you come here today? あなたは今日ここまでどのようにして来ましたか。

○ WhatやHowを使ったさまざまな疑問文

What time is Peter arriving? ピーターは<u>何時に</u>着きますか。

What sports do you like to watch? あなたは<u>どのスポーツ</u>を見ることが好きですか。

How much is this laptop? このノートパソコンは<u>いくら</u>ですか。

How many apps do you have on your smartphone?
あなたのスマートフォンには<u>いくつ</u>アプリが入っていますか。

How old is your dog? あなたの犬は<u>何歳</u>ですか。

How long is this racetrack? この競技トラックの<u>長さはどのくらい</u>ですか。

How far is your office from here? ここからあなたの会社まで<u>どのくらい遠い</u>ですか。

Grammar Hunt!

Tune-Up Reading の英文をもう一度読み、疑問詞を探して下線を引きましょう。下線は3箇所あります。

Grammar Practice

A （　　）内から正しい選択肢を選び、文を完成させましょう。　　CheckLink

1. (**a.** What **b.** Where **c.** Who) does Tom live?
2. (**a.** How **b.** What **c.** When) time does the bus leave?
3. (**a.** Where **b.** Which **c.** Who) team won the game?
4. (**a.** Who **b.** What **c.** Where) called the police?
5. (**a.** When **b.** Where **c.** Who) did Sally get back from Italy?
6. (**a.** What **b.** Who **c.** Why) are you laughing?
7. (**a.** What **b.** Which **c.** How) long is this bridge?
8. How (**a.** far **b.** time **c.** many) is it to the train station?

B 太字部分についてたずねる質問になるよう文を完成させましょう。

1. A: _____ with?

   B: I had lunch **with my brother**.

2. A: _____ on Mondays?

   B: I have **four** classes on Mondays.

Prepare to Read

空所に入る適当な単語を選び、1～5の表現を完成させましょう。その後、音声を聞いて答えを確認しましょう。　　CheckLink　DL 40　CD 40

1. 暑くて湿度の高い　　　　　　hot and _____
2. 貴賓席、特別席　　　　　　　_____ box
3. 倒れて死亡する　　　　　　　_____ and die
4. 競技の関係者　　　　　　　　race _____
5. 競技失格　　　　　　　　　　_____ from the race

collapse　　disqualification　　humid　　officials　　royal

A 英文を読みましょう。Q1〜3の質問の答えとなる部分には<u>下線</u>を引きましょう。

DL 41 〜 43　　CD 41 〜 CD 43

When was the standard distance for marathon races set?

The International Association of Athletics Federation (IAAF) set the distance in 1921. Until then, the length of marathons varied from 40 km to 42.75 km. The IAAF chose
5　the distance of the unforgettable 1908 London Olympics marathon.

Why was that marathon unforgettable?

Dorando Pietri, an Italian pastry chef, was the first runner to enter the Olympic Stadium on that hot and humid July
10　day in 1908. He was exhausted, and he kept falling down. The Queen of England was sitting in the royal box near the finish line, and many people were afraid that Pietri was going to collapse and die in front of her.

How did it end?

15　Race officials helped Pietri cross the finish line. This resulted in his disqualification from the race. He didn't win the gold medal, but he became a hero around the world. The huge emotion brought by the London Olympics was likely the reason why the distance of that marathon — 26
20　miles and 385 yards, or 42.195 km — became the standard.

Q1

1921年まで、マラソンの距離はどのくらいだった？

Q2

スタジアムに入ってきたドランド・ピエトリはどのような様子だった？

Q3

なぜドランド・ピエトリは金メダルをもらえなかった？

Notes　IAAF「国際陸上競技連盟」　exhausted「へとへとになって」　likely「おそらく」　standard「基準」

B 英文の内容についてまとめましょう。下から適切な語句を選んで空所に書き込み、サマリーチャートを完成させましょう。 ↻CheckLink

> **マラソンの距離が決まるきっかけになったレース**
>
> The IAAF set the standard distance based on the ¹( ) Olympics.

> **ピエトリ選手に起こったこと**
>
> ▶ Dorando Pietri was the first runner to ²( ) the Olympic Stadium.
>
> ▶ It was a hot and ³( ) day.
>
> ▶ Many people were afraid that Pietri was going to ⁴( ) and die in front of the Queen of England.

> **レースはどうなった？**
>
> ▶ Pietri crossed the finish line with the help of ⁵( ).
>
>
>
> ▶ He couldn't win the gold medal, but he became a ⁶( ) around the world.

| enter | collapse | 1908 |
| hero | race officials | humid |

C 英文の内容を正しく述べている文になるよう、適切な語句を選びましょう。 ↻CheckLink

1. The IAAF chose the distance of the 1908 (**a.** London **b.** Paris **c.** Rome) Olympics as the standard for marathon races.

2. Dorando Pietri was a (**a.** professional runner **b.** pasta chef **c.** pastry cook).

3. Pietri became a hero because he (**a.** saved the queen's life **b.** ran a dramatic race **c.** won the gold medal).

Word Collector

Olympic Sports

A ❶〜❽はオリンピックの種目を表しています。イラストに合う語句を選びましょう。

❶ _____

❷ _____

❸ _____

❹ _____

❺ _____

❻ _____

❼ _____

❽ _____

gymnastics	artistic swimming	athletics	diving
rhythmic gymnastics	shooting	table tennis	water polo

B 日本語に合う文を完成させましょう。（　　）には疑問詞など、下線部には **A** で学んだ語句が入ります。

1. 水球チームには何人の選手がいますか。

　A: (　　　　　　) (　　　　　　　　) players are on a _____ team?

　B: There are seven players.

2. 新体操はいつオリンピックの競技になりましたか。

　A: (　　　　　　) did _____ become an Olympic sport?

　B: It became an Olympic sport in 1984.

Would You Like to Be a Pioneer Like Coco Chanel?

動名詞・不定詞

Words to Pictures

次のイラストに合う単語を a～d から選びましょう。　CheckLink　DL 44　CD 44

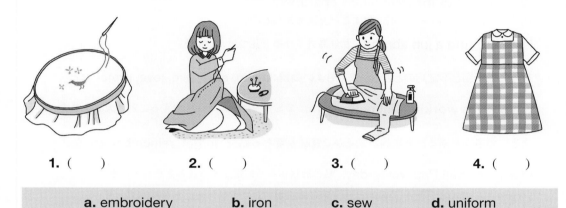

1. (　　)　　　　**2.** (　　)　　　　**3.** (　　)　　　　**4.** (　　)

a. embroidery　　　**b.** iron　　　**c.** sew　　　**d.** uniform

Tune-Up Reading

英文を読み、内容に合っていれば T、合っていなければ F を選びましょう。

CheckLink　DL 45　CD 45

Gabrielle "Coco" Chanel was born in Saumur, France in 1883. Her family was poor, and she had an unhappy childhood. She tried not to remember it. At the age of 12, she began living in an orphanage. She hated wearing the orphanage uniform. She thought it made everyone look "faceless." However, Gabrielle learned to iron, sew clothes and do embroidery there. That was the start of a wonderful career in fashion.

Notes　Saumur「ソミュール郡」　orphanage「孤児院」　faceless「個性のない」

1. Chanel was born in Paris.　　　　　　　　　　　　　　　　T / F
2. Chanel liked the orphanage uniform.　　　　　　　　　　　T / F
3. She thought the orphanage uniform made everyone look the same.　　T / F

○「洋服を作ることが好き」のように、1つの文中で2つ以上の動詞を使う場合、動名詞（-ing）や不定詞（to＋動詞の原形）を使います。

後ろに動名詞が来る動詞：enjoy, finish, keep, mind など

Please keep **practicing** until five o'clock. 5時まで練習し続けてください。
Tom enjoyed **cooking** Japanese food. トムは日本食を作ることを楽しみました。

後ろに不定詞が来る動詞：afford, decide, hope, refuse, want など

We decided **to move** to a new apartment.
私たちは新しいアパートに引っ越すことを決めました。
I want **to find** a job abroad. 私は海外で仕事を見つけたいです。

後ろに動名詞と不定詞のどちらが来てもよい動詞：begin, start, like, love, prefer など

Emily loves **working** out in the gym. エミリーはジムで体を鍛えることが大好きです。

後ろに動名詞が来るか不定詞が来るかで意味が変わる動詞：forget, remember, try など

I forgot **to call** Paul yesterday. 私は昨日ポールに電話することを忘れていました。
I forgot **calling** Paul yesterday. 私は昨日ポールに電話したことを忘れていました。

Jessica tried **to move** the desk, but it was too heavy.
ジェシカはその机を動かそうとしましたが、重すぎました。

Jessica tried **moving** the desk to the window, but it didn't look good.
ジェシカはその机を試しに窓際に動かしてみましたが、あまり見栄えがよくありませんでした。

○ 不定詞を使ったその他の表現
【want＋（人）＋不定詞】＝（人）に～して欲しい
I want you **to stay** with me forever. 私はあなたにずっと私と一緒にいて欲しいです。

【allow＋（人）＋不定詞】＝（人）が～することを許す、～することを可能にする
The new technology allows us **to travel** to space.
その新しい技術により私たちは宇宙まで旅することができます。

Grammar Hunt!

Tune-Up Reading の英文をもう一度読み、「動詞＋動名詞」と「動詞＋不定詞」の組み合わせを探して下線を引きましょう。下線は6箇所あります。toが省略されている場合もあります。

Grammar Practice

A (　　) 内から正しい選択肢を選び、文を完成させましょう。　　**⟲CheckLink**

1. What do you want (**a.** to buy **b.** buying **c.** a と b の両方) at the supermarket?
2. Timmy loves (**a.** to play **b.** playing **c.** a と b の両方) with his dog.
3. We hope (**a.** to arrive **b.** arriving **c.** a と b の両方) around 4:00.
4. Mr. Jones enjoys (**a.** to walk **b.** walking **c.** a と b の両方) in the park.
5. I prefer (**a.** to travel **b.** traveling **c.** a と b の両方) by car.
6. Liz decided (**a.** to take **b.** taking **c.** a と b の両方) a computer class.
7. Gary doesn't mind (**a.** to cook **b.** cooking **c.** a と b の両方).
8. She finished (**a.** to write **b.** writing **c.** a と b の両方) her report on Sunday night.

B (　　) 内の動詞を使って、日本語に合う文を作りましょう。

1. ジムとリンダはテニスをすることが好きです。(enjoy)

　――――――――――――――――――――――――――――――――――――

2. 彼らはイタリアンレストランに行きたいです。(want)

　――――――――――――――――――――――――――――――――――――

Prepare to Read

空所に入る適当な語句を選び、1～5の表現を完成させましょう。その後、音声を聞いて答えを確認しましょう。　　**⟲CheckLink**　**⬇ DL 46**　**◎ CD 46**

1. 一晩で有名になる　　　　　　become famous ＿＿＿＿＿＿＿
2. レジャーやスポーツに適した　　＿＿＿＿＿＿＿ leisure and sports
3. 革命的な流行　　　　　　　　revolutionary ＿＿＿＿＿＿＿
4. 彼女のおかげで　　　　　　　＿＿＿＿＿＿＿ her
5. 実用的で手ごろな　　　　　　practical and ＿＿＿＿＿＿＿

| affordable | overnight | suitable for | thanks to | trends |

A 英文を読みましょう。Q１〜３の質問の答えとなる部分には<u>下線</u>を引きましょう。

🎧 DL 47〜49　◎ CD 47 〜 ◎ CD 49

Coco Chanel didn't become famous overnight. In 1901, at the age of 18, she began working as a seamstress during the day and a singer at night. Nine years later, she opened a hat boutique in Paris and decided to sell only her hat designs.
5 Her big break in fashion happened after a well-known theater actress wore her hats in a play. The actress later modeled them for the famous French fashion magazine *Les Modes*.

Chanel started creating chic but comfortable clothing with traditionally "poor man's" fabrics such as jersey. She
10 designed casual clothing suitable for leisure and sports. She wore pants and a bobbed haircut to social events. These were all revolutionary trends in the 1920s. They freed women from wearing corsets, ankle-length dresses and skirts, and long hair. Her "Chanel suit" became a Chanel trademark
15 and a lasting fashion standard.

Chanel took the comfort of men's clothing and produced styles for women. Thanks to her, women were able to enjoy wearing pants. Her designs were elegant, but also comfortable, practical and affordable. They allowed women to look beautiful
20 and feel free at the same time.

Q1
ココ・シャネルが最初にパリに開いたお店は何のお店だった？

Q2
シャネルが生み出した流行により、女性が身に付けなくてもすむようになったファッションは？

Q3
シャネルのデザインにより女性は美しく見えると同時にどのような気持ちになった？

Notes　seamstress「女性の裁縫師」 boutique「ブティック（小規模の洋品店）」 model「モデルとして〜を見せる」
bobbed haircut「ショートカットの髪型」 free「〜を解放する」 corsets「コルセット」 comfort「快適さ」

B 英文の内容についてまとめましょう。下から適切な語句を選んで空所に書き込み、サマリーチャートを完成させましょう。 ⟳CheckLink

ココ・シャネルが有名になるまで

▶ In 1901, she started working as a ¹( ) and a singer.

▶ In 1910, she opened a small ²( ) shop in Paris.

➡ 有名な女優が帽子を着用、ブランドのブレイクにつながる

シャネルの挑戦

▶ She started creating chic but comfortable clothing with cheap ³( ) such as jersey.

▶ She wore pants and a bobbed haircut.

➡ 1920年代の革命的なトレンドとなった

シャネルが女性にもたらした変化

▶ Women were able to enjoy wearing ⁴( ).

▶ Chanel's designs were elegant, comfortable, practical and ⁵( ).

▶ Women looked beautiful and felt ⁶( ).

seamstress　free　fabrics　hat　pants　affordable

C 英文の内容を正しく述べている文になるよう、適切な語句を選びましょう。 ⟳CheckLink

1. A famous actress modeled Chanel's hats (**a.** in a fashion show **b.** for a fashion magazine **c.** in Chanel's boutique).

2. Until the 1920s, women wore (**a.** short skirts **b.** pants **c.** long dresses).

3. Chanel's designs were (**a.** chic but practical **b.** elegant but expensive **c.** old-fashioned and cheap).

Word Collector

A ❶〜❽ の柄を表す語句を選びましょう。

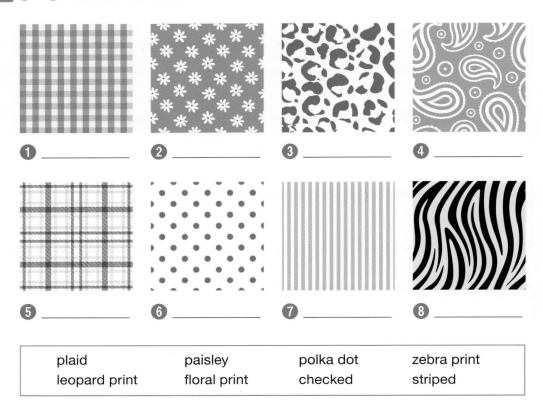

❶ _____

❷ _____

❸ _____

❹ _____

❺ _____

❻ _____

❼ _____

❽ _____

plaid	paisley	polka dot	zebra print
leopard print	floral print	checked	striped

B 日本語に合う文を完成させましょう。（　　）には名詞や動名詞・不定詞、下線部には **A** で学んだ語句が入ります。

1. ミニーマウスは赤い水玉柄のドレスを 1928 年に着始めました。

Minnie Mouse started (　　　　　　　) a red _____

(　　　　　　　) in 1928.

2. 彼女はストライプのシャツと花柄のスカートを買いたいです。

She wants (　　　　　　) (　　　　　　) a _____

(　　　　　　) and a _____ (　　　　　　).

58

What Will Space Travel Be Like in the Future?

未来形

Words to Pictures

次のイラストに合う語句をa〜dから選びましょう。　CheckLink　DL 50　CD 50

1. (　　)　　　　**2.** (　　)　　　　**3.** (　　)　　　　**4.** (　　)

a. go on vacation　　**b.** enter space　　**c.** plan a tour　　**d.** take transportation

Tune-Up Reading

英文を読み、内容に合っていればT、合っていなければFを選びましょう。

CheckLink　DL 51　CD 51

Someday people are going to go on vacations to outer space. Some companies are already planning tours. Trips will be very expensive at first. However, the cost will decrease quickly as demand grows. The first trips will see tourists enter space and return to Earth in only a few minutes. One day, however, people will travel to the Moon and beyond. What kind of transportation is going to take them there?

Notes　demand「需要」　beyond「〜を超えて」

1. Some companies are planning space tours.　　　　　　　　　　　T / F
2. At first, only rich people will be able to enjoy space tourism.　　T / F
3. The first space trips will last for only a few hours.　　　　　　　T / F

59

◯ これからしようとしていることや、すでに決められた予定について表現する場合、willやbe going toを使います。

◯ willを使った表現：「これから～します／～するでしょう」

主語	will＋動詞の原形	その他の情報	意味
I	will buy	a new bicycle.	私は新しい自転車を買います。
You	will pass	the exam.	あなたは試験に合格するでしょう。
It	will be	chilly today.	今日は肌寒くなるでしょう。

[否定文] My father **won't** [**will not**] come home tonight.
父は今晩、家に帰らないでしょう。

Kate **won't** [**will not**] be here tomorrow.　ケイトは明日、ここにはいないでしょう。

[疑問文] **Will** Roger play in the next game?　ロジャーは次の試合に出ますか。

How long **will** it take to finish reading this book?
この本を読み終わるまでどのくらいかかりますか。

◯ be going toを使った表現：「～する予定です」

主語	be going to ＋動詞の原形	その他の情報	意味
We	**are going to** meet	at the station.	私たちは駅で会う予定です。
Our company	**is going to** open	a new restaurant.	私たちの会社は新しいレストランをオープンする予定です。

[否定文] I am [I'm] **not going to** use this headset.　You can use it.
私はこのヘッドフォンを使う予定はありません。あなたが使っていいですよ。

[疑問文] **Are** you **going to** watch the volleyball game on TV tonight?
あなたは今晩、テレビでバレーボールの試合を見る予定ですか。

Where **are** you **going to** go on Christmas vacation?
クリスマス休暇であなたはどこに行く予定ですか。

Grammar Hunt!

Tune-Up Reading の英文をもう一度読み、「will＋動詞の原形」と「be going to＋動詞の原形」の組み合わせを探して下線を引きましょう。下線は6箇所あります。

Grammar Practice

A （　　）内から正しい選択肢を選び、文を完成させましょう。　⟳CheckLink

1. We're (**a.** go **b.** be going **c.** going) to go to the new Thai restaurant tonight.
2. What time (**a.** Sue is going **b.** is Sue going **c.** does Sue going) to arrive?
3. It isn't (**a.** going to rain **b.** go to raining **c.** going to raining) today.
4. Dinner (**a.** will **b.** is going to **c.** will be) ready in a few minutes.
5. Richard (**a.** will come **b.** will comes **c.** will be come) home by taxi.
6. Helen won't (**a.** attending **b.** attend **c.** attends) the meeting.
7. How long (**a.** will it takes **b.** it will take **c.** will it take) to get home?
8. She (**a.** will call **b.** going to call **c.** will to call) you this afternoon.

B 日本語に合う文を作りましょう。　1はwillを使った文、2はbe going toを使った文にしましょう。

1. あなたは2時に家にいますか。（ be at home ）

_____

2. あなたはパーティに何を着ていく予定ですか。（ wear ）

_____ to the party?

Prepare to Read

空所に入る適当な語句を選び、1〜5の表現を完成させましょう。その後、音声を聞いて答えを確認しましょう。　⟳CheckLink　⬇ DL 52　◉ CD 52

1. 特別に作られた宇宙ステーション　　a specially-built _____
2. 4分の1の距離　　　　　　　　　　one-quarter _____
3. ケーブルを上り下りする　　　　　_____ a cable
4. 強いだけでなく軽量の　　　　　　_____ but also lightweight
5. 貨物を宇宙に送る　　　　　　　　_____ into space

run up and down　send cargo　space station　the distance　not only strong

Enjoy Reading

A 英文を読みましょう。Q1〜3の質問の答えとなる部分には<u>下線</u>を引きましょう。

🎧 DL 53〜55　◎ CD 53 〜 ◎ CD 55

A Japanese company announced that it is going to build an elevator that will take people to outer space! The elevator will travel to a specially-built space station almost 100,000 km above the Earth. That's about one-quarter the distance
5　between Earth and the Moon. The elevator will carry 30 people, and the trip will take seven days. The company hopes to complete it by 2050.

The elevator will run up and down a cable. However, the steel cable of a regular elevator won't be nearly strong
10　enough. Therefore, the company is going to make a special cable out of super-strong carbon. Carbon is not only strong but also lightweight. The company is confident in its ability to create one long enough for the trip by around 2030.

The space elevator will greatly reduce the cost of sending
15　cargo into space. It will make space travel safe and easy for researchers and space tourists. One day, people are probably going to live on the Moon or other planets. Maybe the space elevator will take them there.

Note　super-strong carbon「超強力な炭素物質」

Q1

日本の会社が
作ろうとしてい
るものは何？

Q2

特別なケーブル
の素材は？

Q3

未来の人々はど
こに住むかもし
れない？

62

B 英文の内容についてまとめましょう。下から適切な語句を選んで空所に書き込み、サマリーチャートを完成させましょう。 CheckLink

宇宙エレベーターとは？

① It will travel to a space station almost 100,000 km above the Earth.

② It will carry ¹( ) people.

③ It will take ²( ) days to get to the space station.

➡ 2050 年完成を目指す！

宇宙エレベーターの仕組み

The elevator will run up and down a ³( ).

 問 題 点

The steel cable of a regular elevator won't be ⁴( ) enough.

➡ 2030 年までに特別なケーブルを開発予定

宇宙エレベーターにより未来はどう変わる？

The space elevator...

① will reduce the ⁵( ) of sending cargo into space.

② will make space travel ⁶( ) and easy.

③ might take people to the Moon or other planets.

| cost | 30 | seven | safe | cable | strong |

C 英文の内容を正しく述べている文になるよう、適切な語句を選びましょう。

 CheckLink

1. It's about (**a.** 100,000 km **b.** 200,000 km **c.** 400,000 km) from the Earth to the Moon.

2. Carbon is strong and (**a.** light **b.** cheap **c.** heavy).

3. According to the passage, the space elevator will (**a.** definitely **b.** possibly **c.** never) take us to other planets.

Word Collector

Ａ ❶〜❽は宇宙にまつわるアイテムです。イラストに合う語句を選びましょう。

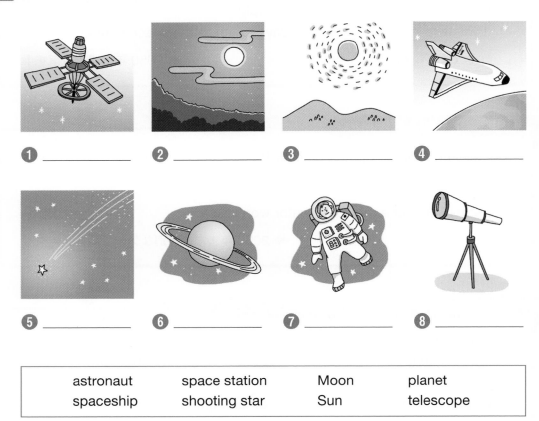

❶ _____ ❷ _____ ❸ _____ ❹ _____

❺ _____ ❻ _____ ❼ _____ ❽ _____

astronaut	space station	Moon	planet
spaceship	shooting star	Sun	telescope

Ｂ （　　）内の単語を並べ替え、文を完成させましょう。

1. いつの日か人類は月に住むでしょう。　（ Moon / live / the / on / will / people ）

Someday, _____.

2. 宇宙飛行士たちは宇宙ステーションで働く予定です。

（ work / are / to / astronauts / the / going ）

_____ in the space station.

What Makes the Amazon One of the Most Amazing Places?

比較級・最上級

Words to Pictures

次のイラストに合う単語をa～dから選びましょう。　CheckLink　DL 56　CD 56

1. (　　　)　　　**2.** (　　　)　　　**3.** (　　　)　　　**4.** (　　　)

a. native people　　**b.** plant　　**c.** rainforest　　**d.** wildlife

Tune-Up Reading

英文を読み、内容に合っていればT、合っていなければFを選びましょう。

CheckLink　DL 57　CD 57

The Amazon Rainforest in South America is one of the most amazing places. It's the largest rainforest in the world — 14 times bigger than Japan! Most of the rainforest is in Brazil (60%), Peru (13%) and Colombia (10%). The Amazon River is 6,400 km long. Only the Nile River in Africa is longer. The Amazon is full of interesting and unique plants and wildlife, and many native people also live there.

1. The Amazon Rainforest is forty times larger than Japan.　　　　T　/　F

2. More than half of the Amazon rainforest is in Brazil.　　　　T　/　F

3. The Amazon River is 640 kilometers long.　　　　T　/　F

Grammar Basics

○ 2つのものを比べて「AはBより〜です」のように表現するときは、比較級を使います。

主語＋動詞	比較級 than ＋比較対象	意味
My suitcase is	**lighter than** yours.	私のスーツケースはあなたのものよりも軽いです。
The green jacket is	**more expensive than** the blue one.	緑のジャケットは青いジャケットよりも高いです。
My father drives	**more carefully than** my mother.	父は母よりも注意深く運転します。
Nancy's drawing is	**better than** Jessica's.	ナンシーの絵はジェシカの絵よりも上手です。

○ 3つ以上のものを比べて「Aが一番〜です」のように表現するときは、最上級を使います。

主語＋動詞	最上級	in/of＋範囲	意味
Central Park is	**the largest** park	in New York.	セントラルパークはニューヨークで一番広い公園です。
This is	**the most luxurious** hotel	in this town.	このホテルはこの街で一番豪華なホテルです。
Eric runs	**the fastest**	in his class.	エリックはクラスで一番速く走ります。
This is	**the worst** experience	of my life.	これは私の人生で最悪な経験です。

○ many/muchや few/littleの比較表現

My brother earns **more** money **than** my father.
私の兄（弟）は父よりも多くお金を稼いでいます。

The theme park gets **the most** visitors in December.
この遊園地は 12 月にもっともたくさんの人が訪れます。

This new toilet uses **less** water **than** older models.
この新しいトイレは旧型モデルより少ない水を使います。

Jim made **the fewest** mistakes on the test.
ジムはテストで最も少なくミスをしました。

Tune-Up Reading の英文をもう一度読み、比較級と最上級の表現を探して下線を引きましょう。下線は4箇所あります。

Grammar Practice

A (　　) 内から正しい選択肢を選び、文を完成させましょう。　　CheckLink

1. Rick is (**a.** older **b.** more old **c.** more older) than Donald.
2. Health is (**a.** important **b.** more important **c.** the most important) than money.
3. Jane's cooking is (**a.** better **b.** good **c.** more good) than Betty's cooking.
4. The Pacific is the (**a.** biggest **b.** most biggest **c.** most big) ocean.
5. February is (**a.** shortest **b.** shortest the **c.** the shortest) month of the year.
6. This is the (**a.** bad **b.** worst **c.** worse) time of year to travel.
7. Emily works (**a.** quickly than **b.** more quickly than **c.** more than quickly) Kate.
8. Of all the girls in the class, Sandra sings (**a.** beautiful **b.** the most beautiful **c.** the most beautifully).

B 日本語に合う文を作りましょう。

1. ニューヨークはロンドンより大きいです。

_____

2. これはこの街でもっとも高いレストランです。

_____

Prepare to Read

空所に入る適当な語句を選び、1〜5の表現を完成させましょう。その後、音声を聞いて答えを確認しましょう。　　CheckLink　DL 58　CD 58

1. 地球の肺　　　　　　　　　　the _____ of the Earth
2. 〜のおかげで　　　　　　　　_____ ~
3. 〜キロまでの重さになる　　　weigh _____ ~ kilograms
4. 森の中を通って　　　　　　　_____ the forest
5. 〜との交流を持たない　　　　have no _____ with ~

| through | contact | lungs | thanks to | up to |

67

A 英文を読みましょう。Q1〜3の質問の答えとなる部分には<u>下線</u>を引きましょう。

DL 59 ~ 61　　CD 59 ~ CD 61

People sometimes call the Amazon "the lungs of the Earth." It produces a lot of the world's oxygen. This is thanks to 40,000 different types of plants, including around 40 billion trees. The top branches and leaves of the tallest trees form a
5　huge canopy. The ground below is almost totally dark. Some of the most important and useful products come from Amazonian plants, such as medicines, food and cosmetics.

About 20% of the world's animals live in the Amazon. One is the green anaconda, the heaviest and most powerful
10　snake. Some grow to be nine meters long and weigh up to 250 kilograms. Another is the Amazon river dolphin, one of the most adorable creatures you'll ever see. These dolphins are pink, and some are larger than humans. The black howler monkey is louder than any other animal in the Amazon. Its
15　howl travels 5 km through the forest.

Thirty million people also live in the Amazon, including 250,000 Amazon natives. They belong to about 50 tribes, speak 170 different languages, and have no contact with the modern world.

Q1

人々はアマゾンを何と呼んでいる？

Q2

アマゾンカワイルカの色は？

Q3

アマゾン先住民の人口は？

Notes　canopy「天蓋（森林の上層部のこと）」　green anaconda「オオアナコンダ」　Amazon river dolphin「アマゾンカワイルカ」　black howler monkey「クロホエザル」　howl「遠吠え」　tribes「部族」

68

B 英文の内容についてまとめましょう。下から適切な語句を選んで空所に書き込み、サマリーチャートを完成させましょう。　**CheckLink**

アマゾンは「地球の肺」と呼ばれている

It produces a lot of the world's [1](　　　　　　　).

なぜそれが可能なのか？… It has 40 billion [2](　　　　　　　).

Some of the most important and useful products come from Amazonian plants.

➡ たとえば、薬・食べ物・化粧品など

アマゾンの豊かな生態系

▶ The green anaconda is the [3](　　　　　　　) and most powerful snake.

▶ The Amazon river dolphin is one of the most [4](　　　　　　) creatures.

▶ The black howler monkey is [5](　　　　　　) than any other animal in the Amazon.

アマゾンに暮らす 3,000 万の人々

▶ 250,000 Amazon natives belong to about 50 tribes.

▶ They speak [6](　　　　　　) different languages.

| trees | 170 | adorable | heaviest | louder | oxygen |

C 英文の内容を正しく述べている文になるよう、適切な語句を選びましょう。　**CheckLink**

1. The ground below the Amazon canopy doesn't get much (**a.** light **b.** oxygen **c.** water).

2. The howl of the black howler monkey travels (**a.** 500 **b.** 1,500 **c.** 5,000) meters through the forest.

3. The Amazon natives (**a.** guide tourists **b.** all live together **c.** do not interact with the outside world).

Word Collector

Natural Features of the Earth

A ❶〜❽のイラストにある地形を表す単語を選びましょう。

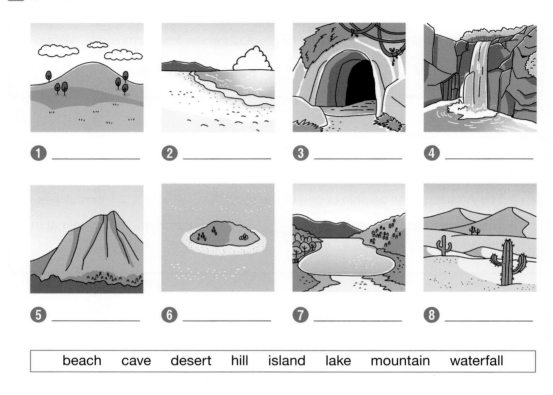

❶ _____

❷ _____

❸ _____

❹ _____

❺ _____

❻ _____

❼ _____

❽ _____

| beach | cave | desert | hill | island | lake | mountain | waterfall |

B Aで学んだ語句と（　　）内の形容詞を使って、比較級の文を完成させましょう。
3についてはあなたの考えを書きましょう。

1. 山・丘（high）：

A mountain is _____ than a _____ .

2. 砂漠・洞窟（hot）：

A _____ .

3. 浜・滝（interesting）：

I think _____ .

Who Can Be a YouTuber?

11

助動詞

Words to Pictures

次のイラストに合う単語をa～dから選びましょう。　ⓒCheckLink　🎧 DL 62　◉ CD 62

1. (　　)　　　　**2.** (　　)　　　　**3.** (　　)　　　　**4.** (　　)

a. elephant　　　**b.** second　　　**c.** trunk　　　**d.** zoo

Tune-Up Reading

英文を読み、内容に合っていればT、合っていなければFを選びましょう。

ⓒCheckLink　🎧 DL 63　◉ CD 63

In 2005, YouTube co-creator Jawed Karim uploaded the first YouTube video, "Me at the zoo." He stood by the elephants and said they had "really, really, really long trunks." The video lasted only 18 seconds. No one thought then that YouTube could become so successful. Today, people watch more than four billion YouTube videos every day. For this, YouTube must have thousands of content creators, or YouTubers. You can become one, too.

Note　co-creator「共同制作者」

1. Jawed Karim downloaded the first YouTube video.　　　　　　　T / F
2. Mr. Karim's video was less than one minute long.　　　　　　　T / F
3. YouTubers are people who watch YouTube videos.　　　　　　　T / F

○ 「〜できる」「〜かもしれない」「〜しなければならない」のように、動詞に意味を付け加えるとき、助動詞を使います。

	助動詞	例文
能力	**can/could** 〜できる／できた	Jim **can** speak five languages. ジムは5か国語を話せます。 We **couldn't** get to the top of the mountain. 私たちは山頂まで行くことができませんでした。
可能性	**may/might** 〜かもしれない	It **may** snow this afternoon. 今日の午後、雪が降るかもしれません。 Ron and his wife **might** visit us next weekend. ロンと彼の奥さんが来週末私たちを訪ねるかもしれません。
義務	**must/have to** 〜しなければならない ※過去を表すときはhad to を使う	I **must** finish this report today. 私は今日、このレポートを仕上げなければなりません。 We **had to** hurry to catch the last train. 私たちは終電に乗るために急がなければなりませんでした。
	should/ought to 〜すべき	You **should** be more careful when you are driving. 運転しているとき、あなたはもっと注意すべきです。 You **ought to** study more to pass the exam. 試験に受かるために、あなたはもっと勉強すべきです。

[否定文] You **must not [mustn't]** walk on the grass. 芝生の上を歩いてはいけません。
You **don't have to** cook dinner tonight. 今夜は夕食を作る必要はありません。
[疑問文] **Can** you come to the meeting tomorrow? あなたは明日の会議に来られますか。
Do I **have to** work on weekends? 私は週末の間も働かなければなりませんか。

○ 色々な意味を表す助動詞
You **may** leave the room now. 部屋を出てもかまいません。[許可]
Could I ask you some questions? いくつか質問してもよろしいですか。[許可]
The children **must** be tired after walking so far.
とても長い距離を歩いたので、子どもたちは疲れているに違いありません。[推量]

Tune-Up Reading の英文をもう一度読み、助動詞を探して下線を引きましょう。下線は3箇所あります。

Grammar Practice

A (　　) 内から正しい選択肢を選び、文を完成させましょう。　　⟲CheckLink

1. Can you (**a.** run **b.** running **c.** to run) fast?
2. It (**a.** may be snows **b** may snowing **c.** may snow) today.
3. I (**a.** should **b.** have **c.** must) to finish my report by Friday.
4. You (**a.** must not **b.** should not to **c.** don't must) miss next week's class.
5. Did you (**a.** has to **b.** have to **c.** must) work late yesterday?
6. Where (**a.** should we go **b.** we should go **c.** should we to go) for lunch?
7. People (**a.** must not **b.** shouldn't **c.** don't have) to leave tips in Japan.
8. You (**a.** should **b.** ought **c.** might) to see a doctor.

B 日本語に合う文を作りましょう。

1. あなたはピアノを弾くことができますか。

_____

2. 私たちは今日は学校に行かなくてもよいです。

_____

Prepare to Read

空所に入る適当な単語を選び、１〜５の表現を完成させましょう。その後、音声を聞いて答えを確認しましょう。　⟲CheckLink ⬇DL 64 ◉CD 64

1. 動画投稿サイト　　_____ website
2. 数百ドル　　_____ hundred dollars
3. ブランドや製品を宣伝する　　_____ a brand or product
4. 会社に支払いを請求する　　_____ companies
5. 踏み石（成功などへの手段）　　_____ stone

| charge | promote | several | stepping | video-sharing |

Enjoy Reading

A 英文を読みましょう。Q 1～3の質問の答えとなる部分には<u>下線</u>を引きましょう。

DL 65~ 67　　CD 65 ～ CD 67

YouTube is a video-sharing website with over 1.8 billion users worldwide. Anyone with an Internet connection can share their videos on YouTube. There's a YouTube channel for almost every interest. To become a YouTuber, a person should
5　make and appear in videos regularly and get people to watch them. You don't have to have a special talent, and you can even make money. For example, one YouTuber earns millions of dollars a year by making videos of herself eating.

Most YouTubers make money through advertisements.
10　Advertisers pay about 10 cents for 100 views. That may not sound like much, but some YouTubers might earn several hundred dollars a week this way. The most popular YouTubers receive money from large companies to promote a brand or product. They charge companies $10 to $50 for every
15　one thousand views.

Some YouTubers use YouTube as a stepping stone to bigger and better things such as acting and singing careers. Justin Bieber may be the most famous, and luckiest, YouTuber of all time. A talent manager accidentally clicked on the young
20　teenager's video from a local singing contest, and "Bieber Fever" was born.

Notes　advertisements「広告」　of all time「史上もっとも～な」

Q1

この文章で取り上げられている動画投稿サイトの名前は？

Q2

ユーチューバーの資金源は？

Q3

ユーチューブから誕生した有名歌手は？

B 英文の内容についてまとめましょう。下から適切な語句を選んで空所に書き込み、サマリーチャートを完成させましょう。 ↻CheckLink

ユーチューバーになる方法

▶ A person should make and appear in ¹( ) regularly and get people to watch them.

▶ You don't have to have a special ²( ).

ユーチューバーの資金源

▶ Advertisers pay about ³( ) cents for 100 views.

▶ Large companies pay the most popular YouTubers money to ⁴( ) a brand or product.

ユーチューバーからスター誕生!

▶ For some people, YouTube is a ⁵( ) to future success.

▶ The luckiest YouTuber of all time may be ⁶( ).

→ A talent manager accidentally saw his video on YouTube.

stepping stone	videos	10
talent	Justin Bieber	promote

C 英文の内容を正しく述べている文になるよう、適切な語句を選びましょう。 ↻CheckLink

1. YouTube has over (**a.** 18,000,000 **b.** 180,000,000 **c.** 1,800,000,000) users around the world.

2. The most popular YouTubers charge companies $10 to $50 for every (**a.** one hundred **b.** one thousand **c.** ten thousand) views.

3. "Bieber Fever" was born because (**a.** Bieber performed on a famous TV program **b.** Bieber's first CD was popular **c.** a talent agent saw Bieber's video by chance).

Word Collector

Job Fair

A 囲み内の語尾に er / or / ist / ian のいずれかをつけて職業を表す単語を作り、4つに分類しましょう。

bank---	comed---	conduct---	dent---	farm---	illustrat---
journal---	lawy---	librar---	music---	photograph---	
pian---	politic---	profess---	scient---	translat---	

---er	---or	---ist	---ian
(waiter)	(doctor)	(artist)	(magician)
_____	_____	_____	_____
_____	_____	_____	_____
_____	_____	_____	_____
_____	_____	_____	_____

B (　　) 内の単語を並べ替え、文を完成させましょう。

1. 科学者は不注意な過ちを犯してはなりません。

(mistakes / careless / scientist / make / not / must)

A _____.

2. 農家の人は毎日早起きしなければなりません。

(get / to / day / early / up / has / farmer / every)

A _____.

76

What Have Plastics Done to Our Oceans?

現在完了形

Words to Pictures

次のイラストに合う語句をa〜dから選びましょう。 CheckLink DL 68 CD 68

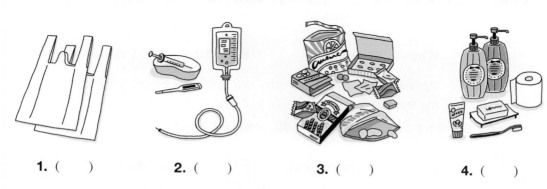

1. (   ) **2.** (   ) **3.** (   ) **4.** (   )

a. food packaging   **c.** household goods
b. grocery bags   **d.** medical devices

Tune-Up Reading

英文を読み、内容に合っていればT、合っていなければFを選びましょう。

CheckLink DL 69 CD 69

Plastics have been around for over 100 years. They have changed how we live, mostly in positive ways. Today we find plastics in everything from cars to household goods to medical devices. Disposable plastics such as bottles, drinking straws, food packaging and grocery bags have brought great convenience to people. These single-use plastics, however, have also caused great harm to our oceans.

1. Plastics have a history of more than one thousand years.   T / F
2. Another way of saying disposable plastics is single-use plastics.   T / F
3. Plastics have damaged our oceans.   T / F

○ 今までに経験したことや、ずっと続けていること、やり終えたことについて述べるとき、現在完了形（have/has＋過去分詞）を使います。

○ 過去形と現在完了形の違い

過去形	I <u>watched</u> "Lion King" yesterday.	私は昨日「ライオンキング」を観ました。
現在完了形 （経験）	I **have watched** "Lion King" three times.	私は今までに3回「ライオンキング」を観たことがあります。

▶経験の文で用いられることが多い語句：once「一度」、many times「何回も」、never「一度も～ない」、ever「（疑問文で）これまでに」、before「以前」など

過去形	We <u>lived</u> in New York.	私たちはニューヨークに住んでいました。
現在完了形 （継続）	We **have lived** in New York for five years.	私たちはニューヨークに5年間住んでいます。 ※ 現在もニューヨークに住んでいる。

▶継続の文で用いられることが多い語句：for「～の間」、since「～以来」など

過去形	Amy <u>went</u> to the airport.	エイミーは空港に行きました。
現在完了形 （完了）	Amy **has gone** to the airport.	エイミーは空港に行ってしまいました。

▶完了の文で用いられることが多い語句：already「すでに」、yet「（疑問文で）もう、（否定文で）まだ」

[否定文] I **haven't** [**have not**] **finished** my homework yet.　私はまだ宿題を終えていません。

We **have never stayed** in a three-star hotel.
私たちは三ツ星ホテルに滞在したことはありません。

No one **has seen** Mary today.　今日は誰もメアリーを見ていません。

[疑問文] **Have** you ever **been** to China?
あなたはこれまでに中国に行ったことがありますか。

Has Erick already **met** Professor Carter? — No, not yet.
エリックはカーター教授ともう会いましたか。— いいえ、まだです。

How long **has** Ben **practiced** karate? — For twenty years.
ベンはどれくらい長く空手を練習していますか。— 20年間です。

Grammar Hunt!

Tune-Up Reading の英文をもう一度読み、現在完了形（have＋過去分詞）を探して下線を引きましょう。下線は4箇所あります。

Grammar Practice

A (   ) 内から正しい選択肢を選び、文を完成させましょう。 　CheckLink

1. The car company has (**a.** cars making　**b.** made cars　**c.** cars made) since 1933.
2. Have you (**a.** eat　**b.** eaten　**c.** ate) lunch?
3. George and Ellen have (**a.** married　**b.** be married　**c.** been married) for 40 years.
4. The game hasn't started (**a.** already　**b.** since　**c.** yet).
5. How long (**a.** are you　**b.** have you　**c.** you have) had your smartphone?
6. (**a.** Have you seen　**b.** Have seen you　**c.** Have you saw) Amanda today?
7. No one (**a.** has　**b.** hasn't　**c.** have) arrived yet.
8. I (**a.** have ever　**b.** haven't never　**c.** have) gone snowboarding before.

B 日本語に合う文を作りましょう。

1. 私はまだ教科書を買っていません。

_____

2. あなたはフランスに行ったことがありますか。

_____

Prepare to Read

空所に入る適当な単語を選び、1～5の表現を完成させましょう。その後、音声を聞いて答えを確認しましょう。　CheckLink　DL 70　CD 70

1. ゴミになる　　　　　　　_____ waste
2. 最終的には～となる　　　_____ up
3. ～に捕らわれる　　　　　_____ caught in ~
4. A を B に変える　　　　 _____ A into B
5. 問題を解決する　　　　　_____ a problem

| end | get | turn | solve | become |

A 英文を読みましょう。Q 1 ～ 3 の質問の答えとなる部分には<u>下線</u>を引きましょう。

DL 71~ 73　CD 71 ～ CD 73

Today, there are billions of tons of plastic on the Earth. Most of that has become waste. Unfortunately, we only recycle a small percentage of the plastic that we use. As a result, a huge amount of unrecycled plastic waste has ended up in our oceans.

Ocean plastic has killed millions of sea animals, from very tiny creatures to whales. Some have gotten caught in plastic fishing nets or six-pack rings. Many more creatures have died after eating microplastics. Microplastics are very small rice-sized pieces of plastic. Scientists have found microplastics from the bottom of the deepest oceans to ice in the Arctic Ocean. They say they have turned the world's oceans into a "plastic soup."

Governments, companies and consumers have started working together to solve the plastic waste problem. For example, in 2017, 193 countries passed the United Nations Clean Seas agreement to end ocean plastic pollution. Coca-Cola has announced a goal of collecting and recycling 100 percent of its packaging by 2030. As a consumer, what can you do?

Q1

使用済みプラスチックのうち、リサイクルされているのはどのくらい？

Q2

世界の海を「プラスチックスープ」にしてしまっているものは何？

Q3

コカ・コーラが2030年までの目標に掲げたことは？

Notes　billions of tons of ～「数十億トンの」　six-pack rings「飲料缶を6本ひとまとめに束ねるためのプラスチックのリング」
Arctic Ocean「北極海」　agreement「協定」　pollution「汚染」

B 英文の内容についてまとめましょう。下から適切な語句を選んで空所に書き込み、サマリーチャートを完成させましょう。 ⟲CheckLink

世界にあふれるプラスチックごみ

▶ There are billions of tons of [1]( ) on the Earth.

▶ Most of it has become [2]( ). ➡ 大量のプラスチックが海へ…

海洋プラスチックが与える影響

▶ Ocean plastic has [3]( ) sea animals from tiny creatures to whales.

 例 え ば …

▶ Some have gotten caught in plastic [4]( ) nets or six-pack rings.

▶ Many more creatures have died after eating [5]( ).

プラスチックを減らすための対策

▶ In 2017, 193 countries passed an agreement to end ocean plastic [6]( ).

▶ Coca-Cola will collect and recycle 100 percent of its packaging by 2030.

| killed | pollution | waste | plastic | microplastics | fishing |

C 英文の内容を正しく述べている文になるよう、適切な語句を選びましょう。 ⟲CheckLink

1. A very large amount of (**a.** unrecycled **b.** recycled **c.** unused) plastic ends up in our oceans.

2. Microplastics are (**a.** match-sized **b.** coin-sized **c.** rice-sized) pieces of plastic.

3. Almost 200 countries passed the United Nations (**a.** Blue Ocean **b.** Clean Seas **c.** No Plastic) agreement in 2017.

Eco-Friendly Habits

A 1〜8は環境に優しい習慣に関する英文です。(　　) に入る語句を選び、英文を完成させましょう。

1. Turn off the lights in an (　　　　　　　　　) room.

2. Bring a (　　　　　　　) to the supermarket.

3. Don't leave the water (　　　　　　　　) when brushing your teeth.

4. Use LED (　　　　　　　).

5. Don't (　　　　　　　) food. Don't buy too much.

6. Fill up your washing machine with clothes before doing (　　　　　　　　).

7. Set the room (　　　　　　　) to 28℃ in summer.

8. Don't use (　　　　　　　) chopsticks.

disposable	empty	laundry	lights
reusable bag	running	temperature	waste

B **A**で学んだ語句を使って、現在完了形を使った文を２つ作りましょう。

1. 私はこのエコバッグを５年間使っています。

_____

2. 洗濯はもうやり終えましたか。

_____

What Would We Do If We Didn't Have Dogs?

従属接続詞

Words to Pictures

次のイラストに合う語句をa〜dから選びましょう。 🔄CheckLink 🎧 DL 74 💿 CD 74

1. (   ) **2.** (   ) **3.** (   ) **4.** (   )

a. watchdog **b.** police dog **c.** therapy dog **d.** guide dog

Tune-Up Reading

英文を読み、内容に合っていればT、合っていなければFを選びましょう。

🔄CheckLink 🎧 DL 75 💿 CD 75

Dogs are wonderful pets. After a new puppy gets home, it quickly becomes part of the family. Because dogs also have many natural abilities, they are able to help us in a wide variety of ways. If they receive special training, some dogs can become excellent watchdogs, police dogs, therapy dogs or guide dogs. Working dogs have helped us in some very unusual and surprising ways.

1. Dogs have very few natural abilities.   T / F
2. Dogs can do many different kinds of jobs.   T / F
3. Any dog can become an excellent watchdog with the special training.   T / F

83

○ 従属接続詞は2つ以上の文をつなげる働きをします。英語と日本語での接続詞が置かれる位置の違いに注意しましょう。

英　語：I took a bath **after** I ate dinner.
日本語：夕食を食べた<u>後に</u>、お風呂に入りました。

after 〜の後に	Please lend me the book **after** you finish reading it. その本をあなたが読み終えた後に、私に貸してください。
before 〜の前に	John left **before** his friends came to see him. 友だちが会いに来る前に、ジョンは去ってしまいました。
when 〜するとき	Lisa went to school by bike **when** she was a high school student. 高校生のとき、リサは自転車で通学していました。
while 〜の間に	I fell asleep **while** I was watching TV. 私はテレビを見ている間に、眠ってしまいました。
until 〜まで	Let's wait here **until** it stops raining. 雨が止むまで、ここで待っていましょう。
because **since** 〜なので	Ken couldn't buy any souvenirs **because** he didn't have any money. ケンはお金を持っていなかったので、お土産を買えませんでした。 **Since** the weather was bad, the sports festival was cancelled. 天候が悪かったので、体育祭は中止になりました。
if もし	Please call this number **if** you want to contact me. もし私と連絡を取りたければ、この番号に電話してください。
unless 〜でない限り	You cannot get a ticket **unless** you are a fan club member. ファンクラブのメンバーでない限り、チケットを手に入れることはできません。
although 〜だけれども	**Although** I was tired, I couldn't sleep well last night. 疲れていたけれど、昨晩はよく眠れませんでした。

Tune-Up Reading の英文をもう一度読み、従属接続詞を探して下線を引きましょう。下線は3箇所あります。

Grammar Practice

A (　　) 内から正しい選択肢を選び、文を完成させましょう。　　⟳CheckLink

1. He did his homework (**a.** before　**b.** unless　**c.** because) he went to bed.

2. Diane burned her hand (**a.** although　**b.** if　**c.** while) she was cooking dinner.

3. We didn't go to the zoo (**a.** although　**b.** because　**c.** unless) it was closed.

4. (**a.** If　**b.** Unless　**c.** While) I'm late, please start the meeting without me.

5. This medicine makes you sleepy. Don't drive (**a.** after　**b.** because　**c.** since) you take it.

6. Most people get nervous (**a.** although　**b.** since　**c.** when) they make a speech.

7. (**a.** Although　**b.** Because　**c.** If) everyone played well, the team lost the game.

8. You'll never pass the test (**a.** when　**b.** while　**c.** unless) you study hard.

B 下線部に正しい語句を入れて、日本語に合う文を作りましょう。

1. ロンは朝ごはんを食べなかったのでお腹がすいています。

   Ron ＿＿＿＿＿＿＿＿＿＿＿＿ because he ＿＿＿＿＿＿＿＿＿＿＿＿＿＿＿＿.

2. 疲れているときは運転しないで。

   Don't ＿＿＿＿＿＿＿＿＿＿＿＿ when ＿＿＿＿＿＿＿＿＿＿＿＿＿＿＿＿.

Prepare to Read

空所に入る適当な語句を選び、1〜5の表現を完成させましょう。その後、音声を聞いて答えを確認しましょう。　　⟳CheckLink　🎧DL 76　◉CD 76

1. 巨大な焼き串を回転させる　　　　　＿＿＿＿＿＿＿ giant spits

2. 特別な犬種　　　　　　　　　　　a special ＿＿＿＿＿＿＿ of dog

3. ハムスターの回し車に似ている　　＿＿＿＿＿＿＿ a hamster wheel

4. 特定の種類の木々　　　　　　　　＿＿＿＿＿＿＿ kinds of trees

5. 〜を見つけることに優れている　　be ＿＿＿＿＿＿＿ at finding ~

breed	certain	similar to	turn	talented

Enjoy Reading

A 英文を読みましょう。Q1～3の質問の答えとなる部分には<u>下線を引きましょう</u>。

🎧 DL 77~ 79　◎ CD 77 ～ ◎ CD 79

For about 400 years, people used dogs to turn giant spits of roasting meat. The English created a special breed of dog for this purpose. It ran or walked on something similar to a hamster wheel until the meat was cooked. However, this
5　breed disappeared after people started using the automatic spit turner.

What would a gourmet do without truffles? Truffles grow underground near certain kinds of trees. For centuries, people used pigs to find them. Although the pigs were very
10　talented at finding truffles, they also liked to eat them. Now, dog breeds such as beagles are used to hunt truffles. But unlike pigs, if they find truffles, they don't eat them.

The Museum of Fine Arts, Boston is full of precious artwork. The museum uses a trained puppy to protect it from bugs. The
15　puppy sits in front of a piece of artwork when he smells a bug on it. Since the dog started working, he has saved the museum much time and money. The puppy's name is Riley, and he is the cutest museum employee ever!

Notes　roasting meat「ロースト肉」　gourmet「美食家」　truffles「トリュフ」　beagles「ビーグル犬」

Q1
この犬は何のために使われていた？

Q2
この犬が見つけ出す食材は何？

Q3
子犬のライリーはどこで働いている？

B 英文の内容についてまとめましょう。下から適切な語句を選んで空所に書き込み、サマリーチャートを完成させましょう。 **C**CheckLink

ターンスピットドッグ：車輪を回す犬

▶ English people created a special ¹( ) of dog to roast meat.

▶ The dog ran or walked on a wheel to ²( ) giant spits.

トリュフドッグ：トリュフを探す犬

▶ Dogs such as beagles are good at hunting truffles.

▶ Unlike ³( ), dogs don't like to eat truffles.

ミュージアムドッグ：美術品を守る犬

▶ The Museum of Fine Arts, Boston has a puppy to ⁴( ) its precious artwork.

▶ The puppy can smell a ⁵( ) on a piece of artwork.

▶ It helps the museum save time and ⁶( ).

| protect | turn | breed | bug | pigs | money |

C 英文の内容を正しく述べている文になるよう、適切な語句を選びましょう。 **C**CheckLink

1. The dog breed used to turn giant spits (**a.** became a pet **b.** used the automatic spit turner **c.** no longer exists).

2. Truffles grow (**a.** on trees **b.** under the ground **c.** on rocks).

3. Riley (**a.** barks **b.** sits **c.** jumps) in front of a piece of artwork when he smells a bug on it.

Word Collector

Animal Parts

A ❶～❽は動物の体の部位です。イラストに合う単語を選びましょう。

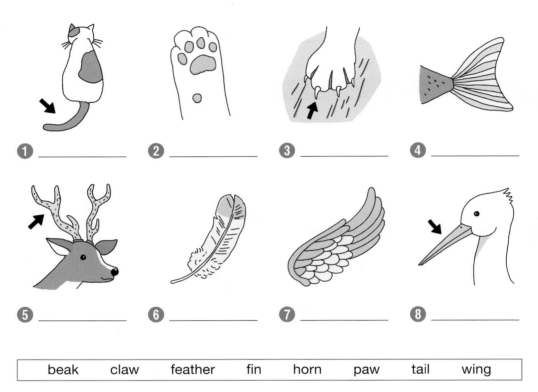

| beak | claw | feather | fin | horn | paw | tail | wing |

B (　　) 内の語句を並べ替え、文を完成させましょう。

1. 犬は興奮したときしっぽを振ります。[しっぽを振る：wag]

(their / excited / tails / they're / wag / when)

Dogs _____.

2. 猫は雨が降る前に前足で顔をきれいにします。

(their faces / clean / their paws / with)

Cats _____ before it rains.

How Was Conveyor Belt Sushi Born?

受動態

Words to Pictures

次のイラストに合う語句を a～d から選びましょう。　CheckLink　DL 80　CD 80

1. (　　)　　　　2. (　　)　　　　3. (　　)　　　　4. (　　)

a. orders　　　b. customers　　　c. a piece of sushi　　　d. sushi chef

Tune-Up Reading

英文を読み、内容に合っていれば T、合っていなければ F を選びましょう。

CheckLink　DL 81　CD 81

Yoshiaki Shiraishi was born in Ehime Prefecture in 1913. In 1947, he opened a standing sushi restaurant in Higashi-Osaka. People were attracted by the low price — four pieces of sushi for 20 yen! The restaurant became popular. However, the sushi chefs were always busy, and the customers often waited a long time for their orders. Mr. Shiraishi wanted to make a shop that was designed for both speed and convenience... but how?

1. Mr. Shiraishi's restaurant was located in Tokyo.　　　　　　　　T / F
2. A piece of sushi at Mr. Shiraishi's shop cost only 20 yen.　　　　T / F
3. Customers were not always served quickly.　　　　　　　　　　T / F

○ ある出来事を語るとき「ケンが窓を壊しました」と言ったり「窓はケンによって壊されました」と言ったり、異なる表現が使われることがあります。人やものが「…される」という意味を表す場合、受動態を使います。

The window was broken by Ken.
窓はケンによって壊されました。

窓が壊された

Ken broke the window.
ケンが窓を壊しました。

ケンが窓を壊した

○ 受動態の文を作るときは、主語の後にbe動詞＋過去分詞を続けます。過去分詞には「〜される／された」という意味があります。

主語	be動詞＋過去分詞	その他の情報	意味
This app	is used	by many people.	このアプリはたくさんの人々に使われています。
This picture	was painted	500 years ago.	この絵は500年前に描かれました。
The rooms	are cleaned	every day.	それらの部屋は毎日掃除されます。

○ 否定文を作るときは、be動詞の後ろにnotをつけます。
　Fresh food **isn't sold** in this store.　この店では生鮮食品は売られていません。
　These bags **weren't made** in Italy.　これらのカバンはイタリア製ではありません。

○ 疑問文を作るときは、主語の前にbe動詞を置きます。
　Is French **taught** in this school?　この学校でフランス語は教えられていますか。
　Was this car **made** in Italy?　この車はイタリアで作られたのですか。

Grammar Hunt!

| Tune-Up Reading | の英文をもう一度読み、受動態が含まれている文を探して下線を引きましょう。下線は3箇所あります。

Grammar Practice

A （　　）内から正しい選択肢を選び、文を完成させましょう。 ⟳CheckLink

1. In Australia, conveyor belt sushi is also (**a.** call **b.** called **c.** calling) a sushi train.

2. The packages (**a.** was sent **b.** were sending **c.** were sent) to the wrong address.

3. The *Mona Lisa* (**a.** is painted **b.** is painting **c.** was painted) by da Vinci.

4. Only ladies' clothes are (**a.** sale **b.** sell **c.** sold) in this shop.

5. Anne (**a.** drove **b.** is driving **c.** was driven) to the airport by her brother.

6. That kind of bird isn't usually (**a.** seen **b.** seeing **c.** saw) around here.

7. Bob was (**a.** told **b.** told by **c.** told to) his doctor to stop smoking.

8. Where were (**a.** these photos taken **b.** taken these photos **c.** these taken photos)?

B 次の文を受動態に書き換えましょう。

1. People speak Spanish in Mexico.

   Spanish _____

2. Someone made her clothes in Paris.

   _____

Prepare to Read

空所に入る適当な単語を選び、１〜５の表現を完成させましょう。その後、音声を聞いて答えを確認しましょう。 ⟳CheckLink 🎧DL 82 ◎CD 82

1. ビールの瓶詰め工場　　　　　　　beer _____ factory

2. 次々と　　　　　　　　　　　　　one _____ another

3. 曲がり角をスムーズに回る　　　　turn _____ smoothly

4. 扇子　　　　　　　　　　　　　　a _____ fan

5. １秒につき〜センチメートル　　　~ centimeters _____ second

corners	per	after	folding	bottling

Enjoy Reading

A 英文を読みましょう。Q1〜3の質問の答えとなる部分には下線を引きましょう。

🎧 DL 83~ 85　　◎ CD 83　~　◎ CD 85

One day in 1948, Mr. Shiraishi visited a local beer bottling factory. There, bottles were moved along a conveyor belt and filled with beer one after another. This gave him the idea for conveyor belt sushi. He made a drawing of his idea and
5　showed it to some machine shops in the area. After much searching, he found a small factory with 20 workers that was willing to help him.

One of the most difficult problems was finding a way to make the conveyor turn corners smoothly. This problem was
10　solved when he saw people holding playing cards one day. It was like they were opening a folding fan. He then designed a conveyor belt to move the same way when it went around corners. Another problem was deciding the speed of the conveyor belt. Although 4 cm per second is common today,
15　Mr. Shiraishi believed that 8 cm per second was the ideal speed.

Finally, in 1958, Mr. Shiraishi opened the world's first conveyor belt sushi restaurant. It was called Mawaru Genroku Zushi and was located in Fuse, or what is now
20　Higashi-Osaka.

Q1
回転寿司のアイディアのもとになったものは？

Q2
白石さんが考える回転寿司の理想的なスピードはどのくらいだった？

Q3
回転寿司の第一号店の場所は？

B 英文の内容についてまとめましょう。下から適切な語句を選んで空所に書き込み、サマリーチャートを完成させましょう。 ⟲ CheckLink

回転寿司の誕生秘話

Mr. Shiraishi visited a ¹(   ) in 1948.

白石さんが見たもの

▶ Bottles were ²(   ) along a conveyor belt.

▶ Bottles were ³(   ) with beer one after another.

➡ 回転寿司のアイディアを思いつく

 問 題 点

▶ finding a way to make the conveyor ⁴(   ) corners

▶ deciding the ⁵(   ) of the conveyor belt

ついにお店をオープン!

▶ The sushi restaurant was called ⁶(   ) and was located in Higashi-Osaka.

| beer bottling factory | filled | Mawaru Genroku Zushi |
| moved | turn | speed |

C 英文の内容を正しく述べている文になるよう、適切な語句を選びましょう。 ⟲ CheckLink

1. Mr. Shiraishi drew a picture of a conveyor belt for sushi and showed it to (**a.** beer factories **b.** restaurants **c.** machine shops).

2. Today, the speed of the conveyor belt in sushi shops is usually (**a.** 4 **b.** 6 **c.** 8) cm per second.

3. It took (**a.** 5 **b.** 10 **c.** 15) years for Mr. Shiraishi's idea for conveyor belt sushi to become a reality.

Word Collector

Sushi Shop Sights

1 a stack of _ _ _ _ _ _
（ stalep ）皿の山

2 vinegared _ _ _ _
（ crie ）酢飯

3 _ _ _ _ sticks
（ hopc ）箸

4 soy _ _ _ _ _
（ caesu ）しょうゆ

5 green tea _ _ _ _ _ _
（ rodpew ）緑茶の粉

6 Japanese horse _ _ _ _ _ _
（ aidhrs ）わさび

B Aで学んだ語句を使って、受動態を使った文を2つ作りましょう。

1. 箸はアジアの多くの国で使われています。

_____

2. しょうゆは、大豆（soybeans）と小麦（wheat）と塩（salt）から作られます。

_____

94

How about Jeans that Have a History?

関係詞

Words to Pictures

次のイラストに合う語句をa〜dから選びましょう。　CheckLink　DL 86　CD 86

1. (　　) 　　**2.** (　　) 　　**3.** (　　) 　　**4.** (　　)

a. denim 　　**b.** boutique 　　**c.** wild boar 　　**d.** Buddhist monk

Tune-Up Reading

英文を読み、内容に合っていればT、合っていなければFを選びましょう。

CheckLink　DL 87　CD 87

Onomichi in Hiroshima Prefecture is famous for making premium Japanese denim.　The denim that is produced there uses traditional dyeing techniques to create the deep blue color called *aiiro* (Japanese indigo blue).　The Onomichi Denim Project boutique sells jeans which are made with this denim.　Before the jeans are sold, however, people who work and live in Onomichi, such as wild boar hunters, fishermen and Buddhist monks, wear the jeans for a year.

1. High quality denim is made in Onomichi.　　　　　　　　　　　T / F
2. Modern dyeing methods are used to make Onomichi denim.　　　T / F
3. The Onomichi Denim Project shop sells used jeans.　　　　　　T / F

Grammar Basics

関係詞

○ 関係詞は、人やものを説明する語句を付け加えるときに使います。英語では、名詞の後に説明する語句が続きます。

英　語： the boy **who** sits next to me
日本語： 私の隣に座っている**少年**

○ 説明を付け加える名詞が人の場合はwho [that]を、それ以外の場合はthat [which]を使います。

名詞	名詞についての説明	意味
the photographer	**who** took this picture	この写真を撮った写真家
stories	**that** have happy endings	ハッピーエンドの（を持つ）物語

The photographer **who** took this picture won an award.
この写真を撮った写真家は賞をとりました。

My sister likes stories **that** have happy endings.
私の妹（姉）はハッピーエンドの物語が好きです。

Many students **whose** first language is not Japanese study at this school.
母語が日本語ではないたくさんの学生たちが、この学校で学んでいます。

○ 場所、時、理由を表す名詞に説明を付け加える場合は、where / when / whyを使うことができます。

名詞	名詞についての説明	意味
the restaurant	**where** we had lunch	私たちが昼食を食べたレストラン
the day	**when** I first met you	私があなたに初めて会った日
the reason	**why** you didn't reply to my message	あなたが私のメッセージに返信しなかった理由

The restaurant **where** we had lunch was featured on TV.
私たちが昼食を食べたレストランがテレビで紹介されました。

I clearly remember the day **when** I first met you.
私があなたに初めて会った日をはっきりと覚えています。

I just want to know the reason **why** you didn't reply to my message.
私はあなたが私のメッセージに返信しなかった理由を知りたいだけなのです。

Grammar Hunt!

Tune-Up Reading の英文をもう一度読み、関係詞を探して下線を引きましょう。下線は3箇所あります。

Grammar Practice

A （　　）内から正しい選択肢を選び、文を完成させましょう。 ⟲ CheckLink

1. The swimmer (**a.** which　**b.** who　**c.** whose) won the race trained hard.
2. The hair dryer (**a.** that　**b.** where　**c.** when) I bought yesterday doesn't work.
3. We went to a café (**a.** when　**b.** who　**c.** which) makes excellent coffee.
4. This is the place (**a.** that　**b.** where　**c.** who) Bob and Elaine first met.
5. I have a friend (**a.** who　**b.** who's　**c.** whose) father is a famous actor.
6. Do you remember the time (**a.** when　**b.** where　**c.** which) we got lost in New York?
7. The driver (**a.** that　**b.** which　**c.** who's) hit the cyclist was very careless.
8. Tell me the reason (**a.** where　**b.** who　**c.** why) you were late.

B （　　）内の関係詞を使って、2つの文を1つにつなげましょう。

1. The woman lives next door. She is friendly. (who)

   ➡ The woman _____ is friendly.

2. This is the book. I bought it yesterday. (that)

   ➡ This is the book _____.

Prepare to Read

空所に入る適当な単語を選び、1～5の表現を完成させましょう。その後、音声を聞いて答えを確認しましょう。 ⟲ CheckLink 🎧 DL 88 ◎ CD 88

1. ～の証拠を残す　　　　　 _____ evidence of ~
2. ミーティングを行う　　　 _____ meetings
3. ～にタグをとりつける　　 _____ tags on ~
4. ～の2倍の　　　　　　　 _____ as much as ~
5. 歴史の一片を買う　　　　 _____ a piece of history

keep	buy	hold	twice	put

97

A 英文を読みましょう。Q１〜３の質問の答えとなる部分には<u>下線を引きましょう</u>。

🎧 DL 89~91　◎ CD 89 ~ ◎ CD 91

How does the Onomichi Denim Project work? Two pairs of new jeans are given to each of around 100 volunteers who promise to wear them almost every day for a year. Each week, one pair is collected and washed by project workers
5 whose job is to keep evidence of the wearers' life and work. The process is repeated for one year.

The project holds informal meetings once a month. Volunteers of various ages and occupations talk about how the jeans feel and point out places where the jeans have
10 gotten fade marks, scratches, stains, etc.

At the end of one year, all of the jeans are washed, dried and checked carefully for unique markings. Store workers put tags on each pair that show the occupations of the wearers, and then display them in the shop. Prices range from around
15 ¥25,000 to ¥50,000. This is about twice as much as a new pair usually costs. However, people aren't just buying a pair of jeans, they are buying a piece of history.

Notes　fade marks「色褪せ」 scratches「傷」 stains「シミ」

Q1
ボランティアの
人たちがする
ことは？

Q2
ミーティングが
行われる頻度
は？

Q3
尾道デニムプロ
ジェクトのジー
ンズの値段は？

B 英文の内容についてまとめましょう。下から適切な語句を選んで空所に書き込み、サマリーチャートを完成させましょう。 CheckLink

尾道デニムプロジェクトとは？

▶ About 100 volunteers wear jeans almost every day for a year.

▶ One pair is ¹( ) every week, and cleaners are careful to keep evidence of the wearers' life and work.

ボランティアたちのミーティング

▶ The volunteers attend ²( ) meetings once a month.

▶ They show fade marks, scratches and ³( ) on the jeans.

ジーンズが商品になるまで

▶ Store workers put ⁴( ) on the jeans that show the occupations of the wearers.

▶ The jeans cost ⁵( ) as much as a regular pair of jeans.

▶ People who buy these jeans are buying a piece of ⁶( ).

| stains | tags | history | twice | washed | informal |

C 英文の内容を正しく述べている文になるよう、適切な語句を選びましょう。 CheckLink

1. Each volunteer receives (**a.** one pair of new jeans **b.** one pair of old jeans **c.** two pairs of new jeans).

2. Volunteers are (**a.** mostly young people **b.** store workers **c.** people with various jobs) .

3. The store doesn't (**a.** wash **b.** repair **c.** examine) the jeans before selling them.

Word Collector

Clothing Items

A （　　）内のアルファベットを並べ替え、イラストに合う単語を完成させましょう。

❶ （ tevs ）

vest

❷ （ skocs ）

_ _ _ _ _

❸ （ sheso ）

_ _ _ _ _

❹ （ thris ）

_ _ _ _ _

❺ （ stanp ）

_ _ _ _ _

❻ （ krits ）

_ _ _ _ _

❼ （ olvseg ）

_ _ _ _ _ _

❽ （ seteraw ）

_ _ _ _ _ _ _

B **A**で学んだ語句を使って、関係詞を使った文を2つ作りましょう。

1. 赤い靴を買った女の子はジェーンです。

_____

2. 私はぴったり合うシャツを見つけました。［ぴったり合う：fits perfectly］

_____

本書には CD（別売）があります

Reading Link

基本文法で学ぶ大学英語リーディング

2020 年 1 月 20 日　初版第 1 刷発行
2023 年 2 月 20 日　初版第 7 刷発行

著　者　　Robert Hickling
　　　　　臼 倉 美 里

発行者　　福 岡 正 人
発行所　　株式会社　金 星 堂

（〒 101-0051）東京都千代田区神田神保町 3-21
Tel. (03) 3263-3828 (営業部)
(03) 3263-3997 (編集部)
Fax (03) 3263-0716
https://www.kinsei-do.co.jp

編集担当　西田 碧　　　　　　　　　　　　Printed in Japan
印刷所・製本所／大日本印刷株式会社
本書の無断複製・複写は著作権法上での例外を除き禁じられています。
本書を代行業者等の第三者に依頼してスキャンやデジタル化すること
は、たとえ個人や家庭内での利用であっても認められておりません。
落丁・乱丁本はお取り替えいたします。

ISBN978-4-7647-4100-3　　C1082